KB054205

레전드 하루 3분 한국어

3-Minute Daily Korean

English ver.

레전드 하루 3분 한국어 English ver.

3-Minute Daily Korean

2nd Edition published   2024.6.10.
1st Edition published   2022.9.25.

written by   The Calling
supervised by   Colin Moore
edited by   Kim Eunkyung
copy-edited by   Lee Jeeyoung
designed by   IndigoBlue
illustrated by   Kim Dosa
video instructor   Tina Kim
video producer   BRIDGE CODE

publisher   Cho Kyung-a
published by   LanguageBooks (101-90-85278, 2008.7.10.)
address   208 Bellavista, (390-14, Hapjeong-dong)
                          31, Poeun-ro 2na-gil, Mapo-gu, Seoul, Korea
telephone   +82-2-406-0047
fax   +82-2-406-0042
e-mail   languagebooks@hanmail.net
mp3 free download   blog.naver.com/languagebook

ISBN   979-11-5635-192-4 (13710)
Price   KRW18,000

Easily, Happily, and Simply from Today!
Starting Again with *3-Minute Daily Korean*

Speaking - Words and Expressions you must use!

Even with simple words and short expressions, you can
communicate. Contains essential Korean words and
expressions for various situations.

Looking - Pictures to help you understand Korean!

Practice by looking at pictures that motivate conversation,
then use what you've learned. Connecting with images will
aid your learning.

Watching - Three-minute video lectures!

The king of all learning is consistency. We hope your
Korean learning will accelerate with a three-minute daily
investment. Tina's video lectures aim to bring fun to your
Korean journey.

I hope *3-Minute Daily Korean* this book and video lectures
help your Korean be firmed!

Writer The Calling

☐ About this book

안녕!

1
Contextual Cartoons

From ordering at a café to travel and emergencies, you will learn words and conversation intuitively. Study easily and enjoy.

2
Romanization & Interpretation

In order to read Korean right away, standard Korean pronunciations are written in Roman characters.

With the following system, you can practice both reading and speaking at the same time, directly from the page.

3

Practical Conversations & Culture Tips

Learning a language starts by understanding cultural differences. We will present the Korean language through its own unique living culture.

Some differences in Korean restaurants!

A tipping culture is not the norm in Korean restaurants. Generally, most Koreans think the price includes a service charge. As for side dishes, the custom for places that serve a variety of them, such as BBQ restaurants, is almost limitless refills.

Korean meals are basically served with rice, soup, and side dishes, but some high-end Han-jeongsik (Korean Table d'hote) Korean restaurants serve the dishes in a particular order.

In Korea, especially given the sentiment that food should be served with affection, the process is accompanied with plenty of care.

< Best Korean food for foreigners >

1. Bulgogi (불고기)

Bulgogi is one of Korea's representative dishes. It is made from marinated slices of beef or pork, grilled but also stir-fried. The sweet and salty sauce is also enjoyed by foreigners.

2. Galbi (갈비)

Galbi is a kind of rib cut into bite-sized pieces. It is usually cooked by grilling or steaming. Galbi seasoning has a sweet or spicy taste.

4

Video Lectures

Short video lectures of about 3 minutes will assist your language learning.

—

Video lectures are provided free of charge on the Language Books' YouTube channel and blog.

"~주세요" means "give."

YouTube   Google Drive   Blog

blog.naver.com/**languagebook**
www.youtube.com
www.GoogleDrive.com

Search "3-Minute Daily Korean"
on YouTube,
Google Drive, and blog.

5

Text and MP3 Transcriptions

Download full-book transcriptions in text or MP3 audio, recorded with correct pronunciation by a native Korean speaker.

MP3 transcriptions of the video lectures are also available. Listen often and improve your Korean skills.

□ Contents

3

Shopping
쇼핑

4

Traffic
교통

5

Entertainment
문화 생활

6

Travel
여행

7

Daily Life & Emergencies
일상 & 응급

8

Basic Expressions
기본 표현

☐ The 11 Most Common Expressions

1 안녕하세요.
an-nyeong-ha-se-yo.
Hello.

2 잘 가요.
jal ga-yo.
Goodbye.

3 감사합니다.
gam-sa-ham-ni-da.
Thank you.

4 실례합니다.
sil-rye-ham-ni-da.
Excuse me.

5 죄송합니다.
joe-song-ham-ni-da.
I'm sorry.

6

이건 뭐예요?
i-geon mwo-ye-yo?

What is it?

7

이거요.
i-geo-yo.

This (one).

8

여기요.
yeo-gi-yo.

Here you are. / Here it is.

9

도와주세요!
do-wa-ju-se-yo!

Help me!

10

한국어를 못합니다.
han-gu-geo-reul mo-tam-ni-da.

I can't speak Korean.

11

미국에서 왔습니다.
mi-gu-ge-seo wat-sseum-ni-da.

I'm from America.

☐ **Characters**

H 헤더 Heather

M 마이클 Michael

 C Cashier · 계산원
gye-sa-nwon

 Clerk · 점원
jeo-mwon

 Crew · 승무원
seung-mu-won

 Customs Officer · 세관원
se-gwa-nwon

 W Waiter, Waitress · 종업원
jong-eo-bwon

 B Bartender · 바텐더
ba-ten-deo

P Passerby 행인
haeng-in

 Passenger 승객
seung-gaek

 Police Officer 경찰관
geong-chal-gwan

 Pharmacist 약사
yak-ssa

 S Staff 직원
ji-gwon

 D Driver 운전기사
un-jeon-gi-sa

 T Ticket Officer 매표원
mae-pyo-won

 G Guard 보안 검색 요원
bo-an geom-saek yo-won

 A Audience 관객
gwan-gaek

 Announcement 안내
an-nae

 I Immigration Officer 입국 심사관
ip-gguk sim-sa-gwan

 N Nurse 간호사
gan-ho-sa

13

1

Tasty Restaurants
맛집 mat-jjip

H: Café latte, please.

C: What size? / **H:** Small size, please. (medium / large)

C: Anything else? / **H:** That's enough.

여기서 드실 거예요?
yeo-gi-seo deu-sil ggeo-ye-yo?

아니요, 가져갈 거예요.
a-ni-yo, ga-jeo-gal ggeo-ye-yo.

카페

진동 벨이 울리면 오세요.
jin-dong be-ri ul-ri-myeon o-se-yo.

네.
ne.

C: For here? /
H: No, take-out please.

C: Please come and pick it up
   when the buzzer rings. /
H: I see.

Tip. **Who gets a discount on the price of coffee?**

To reduce the use of disposable cups to protect the environment, several coffee shops offer discounts to customers who bring their own tumblers.

[Café Menu 카페 메뉴]

커피 keo-pi coffee

- **에스프레소** e-seu-peu-re-so espresso

- **캐러멜마키아토** kae-reo-mel-ma-ki-a-to caramel macchiato

- **아메리카노** a-me-ri-ka-no americano

- **카페라테** ka-pe-ra-te café latte

- **카페모카** ka-pe-mo-ka café mocha

- **카푸치노** ka-pu-chi-no cappuccino

- **아이스커피** a-i-seu-keo-pi iced coffee

- **핫초코** hat-cho-ko hot chocolate

차 cha tea

- **홍차** hong-cha black tea

- **녹차** nok-cha green tea

- **인삼차** in-sam-cha ginseng tea

- **대추차** dae-chu-cha jujube tea

+ Extra Expressions +

➜ When a waiter/waitress gets an order...

Hot or iced?

뜨거운 거요, 차가운 거요?

ddeu-geo-un geo-yo, cha-ga-un geo-yo?

➜ When there is no iced coffee on the menu...

With ice, please.

얼음 좀 주세요.

eo-reum jom ju-se-yo.

With the coffee over ice, please.

커피에 얼음 넣어 주세요.

keo-pi-e eo-reum neo-eo ju-se-yo.

➜ When you have an added request...

<u>An extra shot</u>, please.

<u>샷 추가요</u>.

syat chu-ga-yo.

_리필 ri-pil **A refill**
_빨대 bbal-ddae **A straw**
_홀더 hol-deo **A sleeve**
_저지방 우유 jeo-ji-bang u-yu **Low-fat milk**
_설탕 seol-tang **Sugar**

No whipped cream, please.

휘핑크림 빼 주세요.

hwi-ping-keu-rim bbae ju-se-yo.

Tip. When you use the '~요' form...

When writing a sentence, if you use the '~요' form, you use '~이요' if the last syllable of the word has a final consonant, and if it doesn't have a final consonant, you use '요.'

e.g. A refill, please. 리필**이요**.
    A straw, please. 빨대**요**.

H: One. (two / three / four) /
W: Come this way.

W: Are you ready to order? /
H: Not yet.

Tip. **The trend of brunch restaurants in Korea**

In recent years, brunch has become a "thing" in Korea with popular brunch zones springing up in the major cities, such as Sinsa-dong and Samcheong-dong in Seoul.

20

H: Excuse me!

H: This one, please.

W: Any drinks? / H: No, thanks.

음식 나왔습니다.
eum-sik na-wat-sseum-ni-da.

감사합니다.
gam-sa-ham-ni-da.

다 괜찮으세요?
da gwaen-cha-neu-se-yo?

네.
ne.

W: Here you go. / H: Thanks.

W: Is everything okay? /
H: Yes.

Tip. How do you say 'brunch' in Korean?

Brunch is a combination of breakfast and lunch. It's the same in Korea where people say '아점 a-jeom,' This is a new kind of word, combining '아침 a-chim (breakfast)' and '점심 jeom-sim (lunch).'

W: Are you done? / H: Yes.

W: Do you need anything else? / H: No thanks. Check, please.

종일 **브런치**
jong-il beu-reon-chi
All Day **Brunch**

모든 브런치 메뉴에는 아메리카노가 포함됩니다.

mo-deun beu-reon-chi me-nyu-e-neun a-me-ri-ka-no-ga po-ham-doem-ni-da.

All brunch meals come with americano.

* 음료 변경 시 2천 원 추가 *

* eum-nyo byeon-gyeong si i-cheon won chu-ga *

* charge for changing beverage : ₩2,000 *

- **프렌치 토스트** French Toast　　　　　　　　7,900원

  peu-ren-chi to-seu-teu　　　　　　　chil-cheon-gu-bae-gwon

  두꺼운 식빵에 생크림과 메이플 시럽을 곁들임, 베이컨과 샐러드를 함께 제공

  du-ggeo-un sik-bbang-e saeng-keu-rim-gwa me-i-peul si-reo-beul gyeot-ddeu-rim,

  be-i-keon-gwa sael-reo-deu-reul ham-gge je-gong

  thick-cut bread with whipped cream and mayple syrup, served with bacon and salad

- **팬케이크** Pancakes　　　　　　　　　　　　19,900원

  paen-ke-i-keu　　　　　　　　　man-gu-cheon-gu-bae-gwon

  시럽과 딸기로 토핑한 부드러운 버터밀크 팬케이크에 웨지감자를 함께 제공

  si-reop-ggwa ddal-gi-ro to-ping-han bu-deu-reo-un beo-teo-mil-keu paen-ke-i-keu-e

  we-ji-gam-ja-reul ham-gge je-gong

  fluffy buttermilk pancakes topped with syrup & strawberries, served with wedge potatos

- **그릴 파니니** Grilled Panini　　　　　　　　19,900원

  geu-ril pa-ni-ni　　　　　　　　　man-gu-cheon-gu-bae-gwon

  베이컨, 치즈, 양파, 토마토를 넣은 통밀 샌드위치

  be-i-keon, chi-jeu, yang-pa, to-ma-to-reul neo-eun tong-mil-saen-deu-wi-chi

  whole-wheat sandwich stuffed with bacon, cheese, onions and tomatoes

- **왕 오믈렛** King Omelette　　　　　　　　　23,500원

  wang o-meul-ret　　　　　　　　i-man-sam-cheo-no-bae-gwon

  달걀 세 개, 버섯, 모차렐라 치즈, 양파, 소시지와 토스트를 함께 제공

  dal-gyal se gae, beo-seot, mo-cha-rel-ra chi-jeu, yang-pa, so-si-ji-wa to-seu-teu-reul ham-gge je-gong

  3 eggs, mushroom, mozzarella and onions, served with sausage and toast

+ Extra Expressions +

➜ When you can't decide what to order...

What's good here?

추천 메뉴가 뭐예요?

chu-cheon me-nu-ga mwo-ye-yo?

What are they having? (as pointing to another table)

저 사람들이 먹는 게 뭐예요? (테이블을 가리키며)

jeo sa-ram-deu-ri meong-neun ge mwo-ye-yo?

➜ Side Menu

How do you want your eggs?

달걀은 어떻게 해 드려요?

dal-gya-reun eo-ddeo-ke hae deu-ryeo-yo?

<u>Over hard</u>.

완숙이요.

wan-su-gi-yo.

_반숙 ban-suk Over easy
_스크램블 seu-keu-raem-beul Scrambled

How about potatoes?

감자는 어떻게 해 드려요?

gam-ja-neun eo-ddeo-ke hae deu-ryeo-yo?

<u>French fries</u>.

감자튀김이요.

gam-ja-twi-gi-mi-yo.

_으깬 감자 eu-ggaen gam-ja mashed potato
_해시 브라운 hae-si beu-ra-un hash browns

메뉴가 정말 많은데!
me-nyu-ga jeong-mal ma-neun-de!

치즈김밥 하나,
떡라면 하나요.
chi-jeu-gim-bbap ha-na,
ddeong-na-myeon ha-na-yo.

선불입니다.
8천 원입니다.
seon-bu-rim-ni-da.
pal-cheon wo-nim-ni-da.

H: There are a lot of dishes!

H: One cheese gimbap and a rice-cake ramen, please. /
C: You have to prepay. The total is eight thousand won.

C: Here's the change, two thousand won. / H: Thank you.
C: Enjoy your meal.

여기, 삼겹살 2인분 주세요.
yeo-gi, sam-gyeop-ssal i-in-bun ju-se-yo.

반찬 더 주세요.
ban-chan deo ju-se-yo.

상추도요!
sang-chu-do-yo!

Tip. Koreans love BBQ restaurants!

Many Koreans like to get together at BBQ restaurants. Their preferred dish is pork belly and marinated pork ribs. A more expensive alternative is beef, rib-eye for instance. BBQ restaurants serve various side-dishes that can be refilled and leafy greens to wrap the grilled meat.

M: Here, two servings of pork belly, please.

M: Please refill the side-dishes. /
H: Lettuce, too!

M: Two servings of marinated pork ribs, please. / **C:** Yes.
C: I'll change the hot plate.

냉면 먹을래요?
naeng-myeon meo-geul-rae-yo?

배 안 불러요?
bae an bul-reo-yo?

고기 다음엔 냉면이래요.
go-gi da-eu-men
naeng-myeo-ni-rae-yo.

한번 먹어 볼까?
han-beon meo-geo bol-gga?

M: Do you want some naengmyeon? /
H: You're not full?

M: People usually eat naengmyeon
after having BBQ. / **H:** Let's try it.

Tip. **Naengmyeon**

Naengmyeon is a chewy
Korean cold-noodle dish,
popular in summer,
especially after eating BBQ.

+ **Extra Expressions** +

➜ When you order other things at a BBQ restaurant...

Two bowls of rice, please.

공깃밥 두 개 주세요.

gong-git-bbap du gae ju-se-yo.

Rice is included with this meal.

공깃밥은 이 메뉴에 포함입니다.

gong-git-bba-beun i me-nyu-e po-ha-mim-ni-da.

A bottle of soju, please.

소주 한 병 주세요.

so-ju han byeong ju-se-yo.

How many glasses do you need?

잔은 몇 개 드릴까요?

ja-neun myeot ggae deu-ril-gga-yo?

Two, please.

두 개 주세요.

du gae ju-se-yo.

Tip. Sprite is cider?

In Korea, drinks like Sprite or 7UP are called '사이다 sa-i-da (cider).' This kind of cider obviously has no alcohol.

C: What would you like to have? / **M:** A cheeseburger, please.

C: Do you want the meal? / **M:** No.

마실 건요?
ma-sil ggeon-nyo?

콜라 주세요.
kol-ra ju-se-yo.

사이다 / 오렌지 주스 / 물
sa-i-da / o-ren-ji ju-seu / mul

사이드 메뉴는요?
sa-i-deu me-nyu-neun-nyo?

애플파이 주세요.
ae-peul-pa-i ju-se-yo.

5분 걸려요.
o-bun geol-ryeo-yo.

00:05

네.
ne.

C: Drinks? / M: Coke, please. (Sprite / orange juice / water)

C: Sides? / M: An apple pie, please.

C: It's going to be five minutes. / M: Okay.

가져가실 건가요?
ga-jeo-ga-sil ggeon-ga-yo?

여기서 먹을 거예요.
yeo-gi-seo meo-geul
ggeo-ye-yo.

총 5천 6백 원입니다.
chong o-cheon yuk-bbaek
wo-nim-ni-da.

신용카드로 할게요.
si-nyong-ka-deu-ro hal-gge-yo.

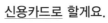

5,600원

체크카드로 /
che-keu-ka-deu-ro

현금으로
hyeon-geu-meu-ro

음료는 직접 하세요.
eum-nyo-neun jik-jjeop ha-se-yo.

Coke Sprite Orange Diet Coke

C: To go? / **M:** For here.

C: Your total is five thousand six hundred won. /
M: I'll pay by credit card. (by debit card / in cash)

C: The drinks are self-serve.

+ **Extra Expressions** +

➡ When you order the set menu...

Combo number one, please.

1번 세트 주세요.

il-beon se-teu ju-se-yo.

Tip. If you find it difficult to order, just select something from the photo menu.

A Big Mac meal, please.

빅맥 세트 주세요.

bing-maek se-teu ju-se-yo.

Upsize the fries, please.

감자튀김 큰 거 주세요.

gam-ja-twi-gim keun geo ju-se-yo.

➡ Special Requests

Cut the burger in half, please.

버거를 반으로 잘라 주세요.

beo-geo-reul ba-neu-ro jal-ra ju-se-yo.

Hold the onions, please.

양파 빼 주세요.

yang-pa bbae ju-se-yo.

M: What would you like to have? / H: Steak and red wine.

M: Excuse me!

W: May I take your order? /
M: One Caesar salad and two steaks, please.

W: What kind of dressing would you like? / M: What do you have?

W: Honey mustard, Italian and sesame dressing. /
M: I'll have Italian dressing.

스테이크는 어떻게 해 드릴까요?
seu-te-i-keu-neun eo-ddeo-ke hae deu-ril-gga-yo?

미디엄 레어요.
mi-di-eom re-eo-yo.

저도요.
jeo-do-yo.

레어 re-eo /
미디엄 mi-di-eom /
미디엄 웰던 /
mi-di-eom wel-deon
웰던 wel-deon

더 필요하신 건요?
deo pi-ryo-ha-sin geon-nyo?

하우스 와인 두 잔이요.
ha-u-seu wa-in du ja-ni-yo.

W: How would you like your steak? /
M: Medium rare. (rare / medium / medium well / well done) / H: Me, too.

W: Anything else? / M: Two glasses of house wine.

W: Red or white? / M: Red.

W: Would you like more wine? / H: No, thanks.

W: Anything for dessert? / H: That's enough.

+ **Extra Expressions** +

➜ When you need something from the waiter...

Salt, please.

<u>소금</u> 좀 주세요.

so-geum jom ju-se-yo.

_후추 hu-chu Pepper

_음료 메뉴 eum-nyo me-nyu Beverage menu

_포크 po-keu A fork

_젓가락 jeot-gga-rak Chopsticks

_앞접시 ap-jjeop-si Extra plates

_계산서 gye-san-seo Bill, Check

➜ When you're wondering about the dishes...

Is the food on its way?

음식이 나오고 있나요?

eum-si-gi na-o-go in-na-yo?

Can I get this to go?

남은 음식 포장해 주실래요?

na-meun eum-sik po-jang-hae ju-sil-rae-yo?

➜ Before the meal...

Enjoy your meal!

맛있게 드세요!

ma-sit-gge deu-se-yo!

➡ When you need separate bills...

Can we get separate bills?

따로 계산할 수 있어요?

dda-ro gye-san-hal ssu i-sseo-yo?

➡ When you want to know about the ingredients...

_육류 yung-nyu meat
_소고기 so-go-gi beef
_돼지고기 dwae-ji-go-gi pork
_닭고기 dak-ggo-gi chicken
_양고기 yang-go-gi lamb
_오리고기 o-ri-go-gi duck

_등심 deung-sim sirloin
_안심 an-sim tenderloin
_갈빗살 gal-bit-ssal rib-eye

_해산물 hae-san-mul seafood
_오징어 o-jing-eo squid
_게 ge crab
_새우 sae-u prawns, shrimp
_조개 jo-gae clams
_굴 gul oysters
_참치 cham-chi tuna
_연어 yeo-neo salmon

M: Do you have beer? / B: Yes.

B: Draft beer or bottled beer? / M: Draft beer, please.

H: What cocktails do you have? / B: Here is our list.

H: A mojito, please. / B: Okay.

M & H: Cheers!

H: Let me get this. /
M: No.

M: I'll treat. /
H: Thanks!

Tip. 건배! geon-bae! **vs 원샷!** won-shat!

'건배' means 'empty one's glass,' but these days in Korea, most people think it just means 'cheers,' and you don't have to drink it all. When someone proposes a toast however, and says '원샷,' it means to down your drink in one gulp. If you're a weak drinker, you can ask to be excused in advance.

[Cocktail Menu 칵테일 메뉴]

- 모히토 mo-hi-to Mojito

  = 화이트 럼 hwa-i-teu reom + 라임 주스 ra-im ju-seu +

  민트 잎 min-teu ip + 감미료 gam-mi-ryo + 소다수 so-da-su

  = white rum + lime juice + mint leaves + sweetener + club soda

- 마가리타 ma-ga-ri-ta Margarita

  = 테킬라 te-kil-ra + 트리플 섹 teu-ri-peul sek + 라임 주스 ra-im ju-seu

  = tequila + triple sec + lime juice

Tip. The edge of the glass is salted.

- 화이트 러시안 hwa-i-teu reo-si-an White Russian

  = 보드카 bo-deu-ka + 칼루아 kal-ru-a +

  크림 keu-rim 또는 ddo-neun 우유 u-yu

  = vodka + Kahlúa + cream or milk

- 잭콕 jaek-kok Jack Coke

  = 잭 다니엘스 jaek da-ni-el-seu + 콜라 kol-ra

  = Jack Daniel's + Coke

Tip. Jack Daniel's is a brand of American whiskey.

< Ordering by phone >

하루반점입니다.
ha-ru-ban-jeo-mim-ni-da.

짜장면 하나, 짬뽕 하나,
탕수육 작은 거 하나요.
jja-jang-myeon ha-na, jjam-bbong ha-na,
tang-su-yuk ja-geun geo ha-na-yo.

Tip. 짜장면 & 짬뽕 & 탕수육
짜장면(jjajangmyeon) is a wheat-flour noodles with black bean sauce.
짬뽕(jjambbong) is a spicy red seafood soup with the same chewy noodles. 탕수육(tangsuyuk) is a pork dish with sweet and sour sauce.

C: This is the Haru Chinese Food. /
M: One jjajangmyeon,
   one jjambbong and a small
   size of tangsuyuk for delivery.

C: The total comes to 25,000. How will you be paying for that? /
M: I'll pay with cash.

C: Can I have your address? / M: Unit 204, 15 Hwa-pyeong-ro.

< Ordering by app >

· 음식 배달 앱 설치 실행 eum-sik bae-dal aep seol-chi sil-haeng
installing and running the food delivery application

· 위치 설정 wi-chi seol-jjeong setting one's position
(예 ye. 마포구 합정동 ma-po-gu hap-jjeong-dong)
(e.g. Hapjeong-dong, Mapo-gu)

↓

· 음식 카테고리 eum-sik ka-te-go-ri /
음식 선택 eum-sik seon-taek /
음식점 선택 eum-sik-jjeom seon-taek
food category / choosing the food /
choosing the restaurant

↓

· 메뉴 선택 me-nyu seon-taek /
추가 주문 chu-ga ju-mun (음료수 등 eum-nyo-su deung)
choosing the menu / adding ordering such as drinks

↓

- 가격 ga-gyeok / 수량 su-ryang price / quantity
  - 주문하기 ju-mun-ha-gi clicking the order

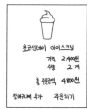

↓

- 주소 ju-so / 휴대폰 번호 hyu-dae-pon beon-ho
  address / cellphone number
  - 요청 사항 메모 yo-cheong sa-hang me-mo
  making a note the request

↓

- 결제 방법 선택 gyeol-jje bang-beop seon-taek
  selecting a payment method

  - 현장 결제 hyeon-jang gyeol-jje on-site payment :
  신용카드 si-nyong-ka-deu / 현금 hyeon-geum
  credit card / cash

  - 앱 결제 aep gyeol-jje payment in app :
  신용카드 si-nyong-ka-deu / 현금 hyeon-geum / 계좌 이체 gye-jwa i-che
  credit card / cash / account transfer

↓

- 주문 완료 ju-mun wal-ryo completing order

< **Online reservations** >

- **예약** ye-yak

  make a reservation

↓

- **날짜** nal-jja / **시간** si-gan / **인원수** i-nwon-ssu

  date / time / party

| 📅 2022-12-24 | 🕐 18:00 | 👤 4 |

↓

- 이름 i-reum / 전화번호 jeon-hwa-beon-ho / 이메일 i-me-il
  name / phone number / e-mail
  - 선택 사항 seon-taek sa-hang option

Tip. '이름' means both the first and last name in Korea.

Michael	Pullman
+82-10-1111-1111	abcd@gmail.com

- 예약 완료 ye-yak wal-ryo
  complete reservation

- 예약 확인 ye-yak hwa-gin
  booking confirmation

< Without a reservation >

W: Did you reserve a table? / H: No.

W: There are no tables available at this time.

H: Put my name on the waiting list, please.

W: Patio or inside? / H: Patio.

H: How long is the wait? / W: About fifteen minutes.

Some differences in Korean restaurants!

A tipping culture is not the norm in Korean restaurants.
Generally, most Koreans think the price includes a service charge.
As for side dishes, the custom for places that serve a variety of
them, such as BBQ restaurants, is almost limitless refills.
Korean meals are basically served with rice, soup, and side dishes,
but some high-end Han-jeongsik (Korean Table d'hote) Korean
restaurants serve the dishes in a particular order.
In Korea, especially given the sentiment that food should be served
with affection, the process is accompanied with plenty of care.

< Best Korean food for foreigners >

1. Bulgogi (불고기)

Bulgogi is one of Korea's representative dishes. It is
made from marinated slices of beef or pork, grilled
but also stir-fried. The sweet and salty sauce is also
enjoyed by foreigners.

2. Galbi (갈비)

Galbi is a kind of rib cut into bite-sized pieces. It is usually cooked
by grilling or steaming. Galbi seasoning has a sweet or spicy taste.
Pork ribs are more common although beef ribs are welcome food
on special days.

3. Bibimbap (비빔밥)

Bibimbap is a delicious, low-calorie dish anyone
who's ever set foot in Korea will know.

4. Samgyetang (삼계탕)

Samgyetang is Korean ginseng chicken soup, a popular summer
stamina food in Korea. It is very nutritious being made of a small
young chicken, ginseng, jujubes, garlic and glutinous rice.

5. Seolleongtang (설렁탕)

Seolleongtang is made from ox and beef bones boiled over for hours. The resulting white-colored soups are rich in protein and seasoned with salt, pepper, garlic and spring onions. A more expensive galbitang is also available.

6. Ganjanggejang (간장게장) & Yangnyeomgejang (양념게장)

Ganjanggejang is crab marinated in soy sauce. It is an addictive food for Koreans.
Yangnyeomgejang is crab marinated in a spicy sauce. Both dishes are made of fresh raw crabs. Those with crab allergies beware!

7. Sundubujjigae (순두부찌개) & Kimchijjigae (김치찌개)

Jjigae is a kind of stew served with rice as usual. Sundubujjigae is a Korean comfort food made with soft tofu, vegetables and chilli paste. Meat (pork or beef), seafood (mussels or clams) or a raw egg may also be added. Kimchijjigae is classic Korean cuisine with kimchi, pork or tuna, tofu, and other vegetables.

8. Gimbap (김밥)

Gimbap is a popular and portable Korean street food. As there are various ingredients inside, there are many types of gimbap.

9. Tteokbokki (떡볶이)

Tteokbokki is everywhere, the Korean street food made with sweet and chewy rice cakes and fish cakes. The original recipe is famously spicy, but these days there are alternate flavors of tteokbokki featuring jjajang (black bean) and carbonara sauces.

Other notable foods include pork belly and jjajangmyeon.
I didn't mention the food that already appeared in the text again.

2

Cellphones

휴대폰 hyu-dae-pon

Please download apps
when you travel in Korea!

10# Buying a SIM Card 유심 사기

M: Can I get a SIM card? / C: Yes. Which plan?

M: Do you have any data-unlimited ones? /
C: How about this one? Unlimited data, calls and texts.

얼마예요?
eol-ma-ye-yo?

7만 7천 원이요.
chil-man chil-cheon wo-ni-yo.

77,000원

이걸로 할게요.
i-geol-ro hal-gge-yo.

네. 신분증 주세요.
ne. sin-bun-jjeung ju-se-yo.

PASSPORT

United States
of America

Tip. When you want to use a cellphone...

For short-term travelers, purchase a prepaid SIM card when arriving at the airport or at a service provider. For longer stays, visit a service provider with your Alien Registration Card and Korean bank book.

M: How much is it? /
C: Seventy-seven thousand won.

M: I'll take it. /
C: Okay. Your photo ID, please.

H: Do you have free Wi-Fi here? / **C:** Yes.

H: Which one is it? / **C:** CAFE-FREE.

H: What's the password? / C: It's on your receipt.

H: It's working!

사진 업로드 해 볼까?
sa-jin eom-ro-deu hae bol-gga?

오, 빠른데.
o, bba-reun-de.

어? 갑자기 연결이 끊겼어.
eo? gap-jja-gi yeon-gyeo-ri
ggeun-kyeo-sseo.

H: Do I try to upload pictures?

H: Oh, so fast.

H: Uh-oh? I lost my internet connection.

+ Extra Expressions +

➔ When you ask about cellphone's plans...

What kind of plan is this?

이건 어떤 요금제인가요?

i-geon eo-ddeon yo-geum-je-in-ga-yo?

➔ When you change the SIM card...

How can I replace my SIM card?

유심 어떻게 교체해요?

yu-sim eo-ddeo-ke gyo-che-hae-yo?

Do you have a SIM card ejecting pin?

유심 교체 핀 있어요?

yu-sim gyo-che pin i-sseo-yo?

➔ When you are looking for a Wi-Fi zone...

Is Wi-Fi available?

와이파이 되나요?

wa-i-pa-i doe-na-yo?

The Wi-Fi is super slow.

이 와이파이 완전 느려요.

i wa-i-pa-i wan-jeon neu-ryeo-yo.

This Wi-Fi works better.

이 와이파이가 더 잘 돼요.

i wa-i-pa-i-ga deo jal dwae-yo.

63

페이스북 해요?
pe-i-seu-buk hae-yo?

네.
ne.

내 사진들을 올려요.
nae sa-jin-deu-reul ol-ryeo-yo.

오, 좋네요.
o, jon-ne-yo.

H: Do you have Facebook? /
M: Yes, I do.

M: I post my pictures. /
H: Oh, good.

Tip. **The most popular SNS in Korea**

Many Koreans use SNS. Of course
Facebook, YouTube and Instagram are
popular in Korea too but many Koreans
like to use native applications like Kakao
Talk, Kakao Story or BAND.

H: Add me on Facebook.

M: What's your profile name? / H: Heather Brown.

M: Let's find you.

M: Is that you? / H: Yes, it's me.

M: I sent a friend request. / H: I got it.

H: I'll add you. / M: Nice! Let's keep in touch.

저기요. 사진 좀 찍어 주실래요?
jeo-gi-yo. sa-jin jom jji-geo ju-sil-rae-yo?

물론이죠.
mul-ro-ni-jyo.

배경 나오게요.
bae-gyeong na-o-ge-yo.

전신 jeon-sin /
상반신 sang-bang-sin

네.
ne.

H: Excuse me. Could you take a picture of me? / **P:** Of course.

H: With the background, please. (a full-body shot / an upper-body shot) /
P: Okay.

H: This picture is blurry.

H: One more, please. / P: Sure.

H: Thank you so much.

+ **Extra Expressions** +

➨ Before taking pictures...

Can I take a picture here?

여기서 (사진) 찍어도 되나요?

yeo-gi-seo (sa-jin) jji-geo-do doe-na-yo?

Can I take a picture of this?

이거 (사진) 찍어도 되나요?

i-geo (sa-jin) jji-geo-do doe-na-yo?

➨ Signs to be aware of...

No photography

(사진) 촬영 금지

(sa-jin) chwa-ryeong geum-ji

No flash

플래시 금지

peul-rae-si geum-ji

Tip. Most museums and art galleries that allow pictures do not permit flash. Before taking a photo, check your camera's set-up.

➔ You can get the best shot if you just move a little!

Move a little to the <u>left / right</u>.

조금만 왼쪽 / 오른쪽으로 가세요.

jo-geum-man oen-jjo / o-reun-jjo-geu-ro ga-se-yo.

Take one step <u>back / forward</u>.

한 발 뒤로 / 앞으로 가세요.

han bal dwi-ro / a-peu-ro ga-se-yo.

➔ What to say to the person you want a picture with...

Let's take a photo together.

사진 같이 찍어요.

sa-jin ga-chi jji-geo-yo.

➔ When you get the best shot...

This is the pic of the day.

이건 내 인생샷이야.

i-geon nae in-saeng-sya-si-ya.

여보세요. 누구세요?
yeo-bo-se-yo. nu-gu-se-yo?

헤더예요.
he-deo-ye-yo.

오! 이거 당신 번호예요?
o! i-geo dang-sin beon-ho-ye-yo?

네, 번호 바꿨어요.
ne, beon-ho ba-ggwo-sseo-yo.

M: Hello. Who's calling, please? / **H:** This is Heather.

M: Oh! Is this your phone number? / **H:** Yes, I got a new number.

+ **Extra Expressions** +

➜ When you want to talk to the person in charge...

Can I speak to Heather?

헤더 있어요?

he-deo i-sseo-yo?

Heather speaking.

저예요.

jeo-ye-yo.

The line is busy.

통화 중이에요.

tong-hwa jung-i-e-yo.

➜ When you hang up the phone or want to call back...

I'll call you back later.

나중에 전화할게요.

na-jung-e jeon-hwa-hal-gge-yo.

➜ Cellphone's mode

My phone is on <u>silent / vibrate</u> mode.

내 전화는 <u>무음 / 진동</u> (모드)입니다.

nae jeon-hwa-neun mu-eum / jin-dong (mo-deu-)im-ni-da.

H: My battery is almost dead.

H: Do you have a power cable? (a portable charger) / M: Yes.

H: Where is an outlet? / M: Over there.

M: I had three missed calls. I have to go, now.

H: How can I give it back? / M: Text me, please.

공원 gong-won /
전망대 jeon-mang-dae /
절 jeol

H: I'm lost.

H: Excuse me. Where is the fish market? (park / observatory / temple) /

P: I'm new here too. Just a moment.

P: Oh, it's near here. / H: Great!

P: Go straight to the crossroad.

P: Then turn left. (turn right)

Please download apps when you travel in Korea!

1. Direction guidance

- Google Maps / Kakao Map / T map / Smarter Subway

- Access maps and information about navigation and public transport.

2. Booking accommodations

- Hotels.com / Booking.com

- Book accommodations at various hotels.
- Save money via discount offers and vouchers.

3. Calling a taxi

- Kakao T

- In addition to taxis, it provides chauffeur services.

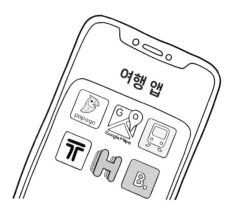

4. Translation

- Papago

papago

- Can translate 13 different languages.
- Can translate language from text, images, sound and more.
- Contains a dictionary.

5. Traveling of Korea

- Korea Tour / Visit Korea / 1330 Korea Travel Hotline

- Helps Korean visitors make the most of their time with information on attractions, food, accommodations, shopping and festivals.

3

Shopping
쇼핑 syo-ping

S: Hello! May I help you? / H: I'm just looking around.

H: Do you have this in black? (white / yellow) / S: Yes, what size?

H: 90.

H: Can I try it on? / S: Sure.

H: Where is the fitting room? / S: Come this way.

S: What are you looking for? / **M:** I'd like some sneakers.

S: How about these? / **M:** Oh! I like them.

Tip. Shoe Size Reference Chart

Korea(mm)		230	235	240	250	260	270	280
US	M	5	5.5	6	7	8	9	10
	F	6	6.5	7	8	9	10	11
UK/AUS	M	4.5	5	5.5	6.5	7.5	8.5	9.5
	F	3.5	4	4.5	5.5	6.5	7.5	8.5
EU	M	38	39	40	41	42	43	44
	F	37	37.5	38	39	40	41	42

M: Can I try these in a 260? / S: Sorry, we don't have that size.

S: Why don't you try them in a 265?

M: They fit. (They are tight / They are loose)

H: I'm looking for toner. (lotion / sunblock)

H: Which one sells the best? / **S:** This one.

H: Is it okay for oily skin? / **S:** Yes, it's for all types.

H: Can I try this? / S: Yes, use this tester.
S: How do you like it? / H: It's a little bit sticky.

+ **Extra Expressions** +

➥ When you talk about size and wearability...

I take a <u>95 / 100 / 105</u>.

<u>95호 / 100호 / 105호예요.</u>
gu-si-bo-ho / bae-ko / bae-go-ho-ye-yo.

Do you have a <u>smaller / bigger</u> one?

<u>더 작은 / 더 큰</u> 사이즈 있어요?
deo ja-geun / deo keun sa-i-jeu i-sseo-yo?

➥ When you want to see something in detail...

Please show me that.

저거 보여 주세요.
jeo-geo bo-yeo ju-se-yo.

➥ When you're asking about location...

Where is the grocery store?

식료품점은 어디 있어요?
sing-nyo-pum-jeo-meun eo-di i-sseo-yo?

Which floor are the electronics on?

전자제품 매장은 몇 층이에요?
jeon-ja-je-pum mae-jang-eun myeot cheung-i-e-yo?

→ When you're asking about products...

Can I get a new one?

새것 있어요?

sae-geot i-sseo-yo?

Sorry, that's the last one.

죄송하지만, 마지막 상품입니다.

joe-song-ha-ji-man, ma-ji-mak sang-pu-mim-ni-da.

It's sold out.

다 팔렸어요.

da pal-ryeo-sseo-yo.

→ When you're checking out discounts...

Is this on sale?

이거 할인하나요?

i-geo ha-rin-ha-na-yo?

It's on sale, twenty percent off.

20% 할인해요.

i-sip-peo-sen-teu ha-rin-hae-yo.

총 4만 5천 원입니다.
chong sa-man o-cheon wo-nim-ni-da.

45,000원

할인 가격인가요?
ha-rin ga-gyeo-gin-ga-yo?

네.
ne.

C: Your total is forty-five thousand won.

H: Is this the sale price? / C: Yes, it is.

세금 환급하고 싶은데요.
se-geum hwan-geu-pa-go
si-peun-de-yo.

여권 주세요.
yeo-ggwon ju-se-yo.

상품과 부가세 환급증 잘 챙기세요.
sang-pum-gwa bu-ga-sse hwan-geup-jjeung
jal chaeng-gi-se-yo.

Tip. Tax Refunds

H: I'd like to receive a tax refund. /

C: Your passport, please.

C: Keep the goods and the VAT refund receipts.

When you purchase goods at Tax Free stores, you can receive tax refund. You have to keep your VAT refund receipts and goods, and you claim your tax refund at airports. You'd better check the website in advance. https://english.visitkorea.or.kr

카드로 할게요.
ka-deu-ro hal-gge-yo.

서명해 주세요.
seo-myeong-hae ju-se-yo.

여기 영수증이요.
yeo-gi yeong-su-jeung-i-yo.

H: I'll pay by credit card. /
C: Sign please.

C: Here is your receipt.

Tip. When you pay by creidt card in Korea...

After you give your card to the clerk, and he/she will have you check the payment and sign. You don't have to enter the pin number.

+ Extra Expressions +

➜ When you haggle the price...

Could you give me a discount?

깎아 줄 수 있어요?

gga-gga jul ssu i-sseo-yo?

➜ When you're wondering about price and discounts...

It's <u>cheap / expensive</u>.

이거 싸네요 / 비싸네요.

i-geo ssa-ne-yo / bi-ssa-ne-yo.

It is not the sale price.

할인 가격이 아니에요.

ha-rin ga-gyeo-gi a-ni-e-yo.

You charged me the original price.

할인 적용이 안 됐어요.

ha-rin jeo-gyong-i an dwae-sseo-yo.

Can I use this voucher?

이 쿠폰 쓸 수 있어요?

i ku-pon sseul ssu i-sseo-yo?

M: I'd like a refund.

C: Can I have the receipt? / **M:** Yes, here it is.

C: Oh, it was a sale item.

C: Sorry, we can't refund these.

M: But it's damaged here. / C: Hmm...

M: Can I exchange them then?

C: Okay, you can get a different one. / M: Thanks.

→ When you return or exchange goods...

I'd like to return this.

반품하고 싶어요.

ban-pum-ha-go si-peo-yo.

Can you refund me the difference?

차액을 환불 받을 수 있어요?

cha-ae-geul hwan-bul ba-deul ssu i-sseo-yo?

You have to pay for the return shipping.

반품 배송비를 부담하셔야 합니다.

ban-pum bae-song-bi-reul bu-dam-ha-syeo-ya ham-ni-da.

Please give me your account number for a refund.

환불 계좌를 알려 주세요.

hwan-bul gye-jwa-reul al-ryeo ju-se-yo.

< **Customer service by email** >

안녕하세요.
an-nyeong-ha-se-yo.

제 이름은 헤더이고, 주문 번호는 12345입니다.
je i-reu-meun he-deo-i-go, ju-mun beon-ho-neun il-i-sam-sa-o-im-ni-da.

파손된 상품을 받았습니다.
pa-son-doen sang-pu-meul ba-dat-sseum-ni-da.

반품하고 환불 받으려고요.
ban-pum-ha-go hwan-hul ba-deu-ryeo-go-yo.

사진을 첨부합니다.
sa-ji-neul cheom-bu-ham-ni-da.

확인 후 다음 절차를 알려 주시기 바랍니다.
hwa-gin hu da-eum jeol-cha-reul al-ryeo ju-si-gi ba-ram-ni-da.

답장 기다리겠습니다.
dap-jjang gi-da-ri-get-sseum-ni-da.

안녕히 계세요.
an-nyeong-hi gye-se-yo.

헤더 드림
he-deo deu-rim

이메일

Hello.
My name is Heather. My order number is 12345.
I received a damaged item.
I would like to return my order and get a refund.
I've attached pictures.
Please confirm and inform me what I should do next.
I'm looking forward to your reply.

Best regards,
Heather

+ **Extra Expressions** +

➜ Other complaints

I have not received my items yet.

상품을 아직 못 받았어요.
sang-pu-meul a-jik mot ba-da-sseo-yo.

I received a different item.

상품을 다른 것으로 받았어요.
sang-pu-meul da-reun geo-seu-ro ba-da-sseo-yo.

I want to get a new one.

새 상품으로 받고 싶어요.
sae sang-pu-meu-ro bat-ggo si-peo-yo.

I want to cancel my order.

주문을 취소하고 싶어요.
ju-mu-neul chwi-so-ha-go si-peo-yo.

➜ Useful words for online shopping

_계정 만들기 gye-jeong man-deul-gi create an account

_주문 ju-mun orders

_개수 gae-ssu QTY (= quantity)

_단가 dan-gga unit price

_할인 ha-rin on sale

_결제 gyeol-jje payment

_배송 bae-song shipping

_예상 배송일 ye-sang bae-song-il estimated delivery

_고객 센터 go-gaek sen-teo contact us

Get the items! (a shopping list)

- **옷** ot clothes

- **바지** ba-ji pants

- **반바지** ban-ba-ji shorts

- **치마** chi-ma skirt

- **조끼** jo-ggi vest

- **양말** yang-mal socks

- **장갑** jang-gap gloves

- **속옷** so-got underwear

- **수영복** su-yeong-bok swimsuit

- **신발** sin-bal shoes

- **가방** ga-bang bag

- **지갑** ji-gap wallet / purse

- 보석 bo-seok jewelry
- 목걸이 mok-ggeo-ri necklace
- 팔찌 pal-jji bracelet
- 귀걸이 gwi-geo-ri earrings
- 반지 ban-ji ring

- 화장품 hwa-jang-pum cosmetics
- 세안제 se-an-je cleanser
- 기초화장 gi-cho-hwa-jang skincare
- 색조 화장 saek-jjo hwa-jang makeup
- 틴트 tin-teu lip stain
- 매니큐어 mae-ni-kyu-eo nail polish

- 향수 hyang-su perfume

4

Traffic

교통 gyo-tong

Korea, the heaven of public transportation!

H: Where is the bus stop? / P: Two blocks from here.

H: This way? / P: Yes.

H: Can I get a bus to downtown there? / P: No. You'll need to transfer.

H: What's the best way? / P: Take the subway.

H: How can I get to the metro station? / P: The nearest one...

P: Just around the corner.

명동 가는 표 한 장이요.
myeong-dong ga-neun pyo han jang-i-yo.

고객 안내 센터

명동 가는 방향이 어느 쪽이죠?
myeong-dong ga-neun bang-hyang-i
eo-neu jjo-gi-jyo?

반대편이요.
ban-dae-pyeo-ni-yo.

Tip. **Get the transfer discount!**

Using a transportation card to take a bus or
subway can get you a transfer discount. Touch
the card to the scanner when you board to pay
the regular fare, then again when you leave.
If you transfer to another bus or subway within
half an hour, it's free. (Make sure you scan when
exiting the bus too!) Additional fares will be
charged depending on the distance traveled.

H: One ticket to
Myeong-dong.

H: Which track goes to
Myeong-dong? /
P2: On the other side.

➜ The way to Seoul Station

Is this the right way to Seoul Station?

서울역으로 가는 길이 맞나요?

seo-ul-ryeo-geu-ro ga-neun gi-ri man-na-yo?

Which line goes to Seoul Station?

어떤 노선이 서울역으로 가요?

eo-ddeon no-seo-ni seo-ul-ryeo-geu-ro ga-yo?

Where do I transfer to Seoul Station?

서울역에 가려면 어디서 환승하나요?

seo-ul-ryeo-ge ga-ryeo-myeon eo-di-seo hwan-seung-ha-na-yo?

Which stop do I get off for Seoul Station?

서울역에 가려면 어느 역에서 내리나요?

seo-ul-ryeo-ge ga-ryeo-myeon eo-neu yeo-ge-seo nae-ri-na-yo?

Which exit do I take for Seoul Station?

서울역에 가려면 몇 번 출구로 나가나요?

seo-ul-ryeo-ge ga-ryeo-myeon myeot bbeon chul-gu-ro na-ga-na-yo?

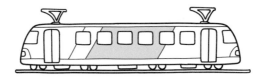

D: Where shall I take you? / M: City Hall, please.

D: Fasten your seat belt, please.

M: A traffic jam!

M: How long does it take? / D: About twenty minutes.

M: Pull over here, please.

M: Keep the change.

< Purchasing a Korail Pass >

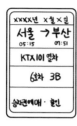

· 예약 ye-yak reservation

· 패스 종류 pae-seu jong-nyu / 출발일 chul-ba-ril

  pass type / departure date

KORAIL PASS Type	KORAIL PASS (2 day use)		
First date of travel with KORAIL PASS	21 ▼	12 ▼	2022 ▼ dd-mm-yyyy

↓

· 개인 정보 gae-in jeong-bo personal information

Name	Heather Brown		
Gender	○ Male ⦿ Female		
Birthdate	12 ▼	12 ▼	2002 ▼ dd-mm-yyyy
E-mail	heather@gmail.com		

↓

· 결제 gyeol-jje payment

⦿ Overseas Issued (VISA, MASTER, JCB)

○ Korea Issued [⦿ Personal ○ Corporate]

PAYMENT >   CANCEL

↓

< Confirm your trip schedule >

- 내 예약 nae ye-yak my reservation
  - 날짜 선택 nal-jja seon-taek choose the travel dates

- 좌석 예약 jwa-seok ye-yak / 좌석 선택 jwa-seok seon-taek
  seat reservation / select the seat

- 예약 완료 ye-yak wal-ryo complete your reservation

Tip. Korail Pass

The Korail Pass is a rail pass for foreign visitors, covering travel by train.
You must purchase the pass in advance (31 days prior to your travel date)
and reserve a seat online or at train stations throughout Korea.
Some benefits are available. (You can also make reservations at
www.letskorail.com or select travel agency websites.)

H: Did you book a seat? /
M: Huh? Can't I ride just holding my Korail Pass?

H: No, you have to book. If you didn't, you can do it at the station.

M: I would like to book a seat to Busan. /
T: Can I see your Korail Pass and passport?

M: Thank you.

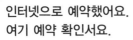

인터넷으로 예약했어요.
여기 예약 확인서요.
in-teo-ne-seu-ro ye-ya-kae-sseo-yo.
yeo-gi ye-yak hwa-gin-seo-yo.

신분증과 운전면허증 주세요.
sin-bun-jjeung-gwa
un-jeon-myeon-heo-jjeung ju-se-yo.

내용 확인해 주세요.
nae-yong hwa-gin-hae ju-se-yo.

M: I booked online. Here is my voucher.

S: Your ID and driver's license, please.

S: Check your rental details, please.

자동 변속기, 휘발유,
내비게이션, 종합 보험.
ja-dong byeon-sok-ggi, hwi-bal-ryu,
nae-bi-ge-i-syeon, jong-hap bo-heom.

자차 손해 면책 제도는요?
ja-cha son-hae myeon-chaek
je-do-neun-nyo?

'고객 부담금 면제, 5만 원 또는
30만 원 부담'이 있어요.
'go-gaek bu-dam-geum myeon-je, o-man won
ddo-neun sam-sim-man won bu-dam'-i i-sse-yo.

'면제'로 해 주세요.
'myeon-je'-ro hae ju-se-yo.

M: Automatic, gasoline, GPS, full coverage insurance. How about CDW (Collison Damage Waiver)?

S: You can choose *Zero Excess, 50,000 won or 300,000 won.* /

M: I choose *Zero Excess.*

Tip. To rent a car in Korea...

You must have a valid International Driving Permit (IDP) or a valid driver's license issued in Korea, and your own credit card.

115

차는 주차장에 있습니다.
따라오세요.

cha-neun ju-cha-jang-e i-sseum-ni-da.
dda-ra-o-se-yo.

차를 확인하시고,
여기에 서명해 주세요.

cha-reul hwa-gin-ha-si-go,
yeo-gi-e seo-myeong-hae ju-se-yo.

S: Your car is in the parking lot. Follow me.

S: Inspect the car's condition and sign here, please.

+ **Extra Expressions** +

→ Confirmations when renting a car...

pickup / return location

대여 / 반납 장소
dae-yeo / ban-nap jang-so

Drop car off at different location

다른 장소에서 반납
da-reun jang-so-e-seo ban-nap

automatic / manual

자동 변속기 / 수동 변속기
ja-dong byeon-sok-ggi / su-dong byeon-sok-ggi

additional driver

추가 운전자
chu-ga un-jeon-ja

fuel policy

연료 방법
yol-ryo bang-beop

_기름 채워서 반납 gi-reum chae-wo-seo ban-nap **full to full**
_그대로 반납 geu-dae-ro ban-nap **full to low**

[Traffic Signs 도로 표지판]

· (일시)정지

(il-ssi-)jeong-ji

STOP

· 진입금지

ji nip-geum-ji

NO ENTERING

· 주차 금지

ju-cha geum-ji

NO PARKING ANY TIME

· 주정차 금지

ju-jeong-cha geum-ji

NO STANDING / NO PARKING

· 양보

yang-bo

YIELD

· 일방통행

il-bang-tong-haeng

ONE WAY

· 최고 속도 제한(50㎞/h)

choe-go sok-ddo je-han
(si-sok o-sip kil-ro-mi-teo)

SPEED LIMIT (50)

· 서행

seo-haeng

SLOW DOWN

· 버스 전용 차로

beo-seu jeo-nyong cha-ro

BUS-ONLY LANE

· 견인 지역

gyeo-nin ji-yeok

TOW-AWAY ZONE

휘발유, 5만 원이요.
hwi-bal-ryu, o-man wo-ni-yo.

결제해 드리겠습니다.
gyeol-jje-hae
deu-ri-get-sseum-ni-da.

창문을 닦아 드릴까요?
chang-mu-neul da-gga
deu-ril-gga-yo?

네, 부탁합니다.
ne, bu-ta-kam-ni-da.

주유 완료되었습니다.
안전 운전하세요.
ju-yu wal-ryo-doe-eot-sseum-ni-da.
an-jeon un-jeon-ha-se-yo.

H: Gasoline, fifty thousand won, please. / S: How would you like to pay?

S: Can I clean your windows? / H: Yes, please.

S: You're all filled up. Drive safely.

< Self-service gas station >

시작 버튼 클릭 si-jak beo-teun keul-rik

→ 유종 체크 yu-jong che-keu
   (고급 휘발유 go-geup hwi-bal-ryu /
   무연 휘발유 mu-yeon hwi-bal-ryu /
   경유 gyeong-yu)

→ 금액 또는 주유량 체크 geu-maek ddo-neun ju-yu-ryang che-keu

→ 결제 gyeol-jje

→ 주유기 삽입 ju-yu-gi sa-bip

→ 주유 시작 ju-yu si-jak

→ 영수증 yeong-su-jeung

Press the start button
→ Check the fuel types
   (High-grade petrol / Regular Unleaded / Diesel)
→ Enter a payment or desired number of liters
→ Payment
→ Insert nozzle
→ Start pumping gas
→ Take receipt

Korea, the heaven of public transportation!

In contrast to the transportation systems of other developed countries, fares are cheap.

1. We recommend buses or subways for thrifty travelers.

As of this writing, a basic adult fare is comfortably under 2,000 won with transfer discounts when rechargeable cards such as Cashbee or Tmoney are used. Purchase one at select banks, subway stations and corner stores.

Major cities are subway friendly. Seoul, Incheon, Daegu and Busan have established systems; Gwangju and Daejeon have single lines with plans to expand. Planning your bus/subway commute is made easier too with electronic signboards that post arrival information.

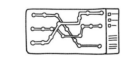

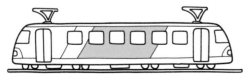

2. We recommend taxis to those who like convenience.

For more personal service, you're never far from a roaming taxi and there's something for everyone. Besides the standard variety, International Taxis offer drivers with specific language skills while the black Deluxe Taxis provide more space and comfort for higher fares. Most kinds can be both hailed on the street or called via phone or mobile app. The call center you connect with might not be English friendly however. Get the full taxi breakdown at *https://english.visitkorea.or.kr* undertransportation.

5

Entertainment
문화 생활 mun-hwa saeng-hwal

G: Open your bag, please.

H: One adult, please. And an audio guide.

H: How much is it? / C: Audio guides are free.

C: You can pick it up on the second floor. / H: Thank you.

127

S: American? / H: Yes.

S: Would you like English? /
H: English and Korean, please. (Japanese / Chinese / Spanish / French / German)

S: Your ID, please.

➔ At the ticket / information office

What time do you close?

몇 시에 닫아요?

myeot ssi-e da-da-yo?

Where can I get a brochure?

안내 책자가 어디 있어요?

an-nae chaek-jja-ga eo-di i-sseo-yo?

Where is the <u>entrance / exit</u>?

입구 / 출구가 어디예요?

ip-ggu / chul-gu-ga eo-di-ye-yo?

입구

➔ When you want to check your bag...

Can I check my bag?

가방을 맡길 수 있나요?

ga-bang-eul mat-ggil ssu in-na-yo?

Where are the lockers?

사물함 있어요?

sa-mul-ham i-sseo-yo?

M: Is this show playing tonight? / S: Yes.

M: Can I get in now? /

S: Not yet. In ten minutes. (in a quarter of an hour / in a half hour)

표 보여 주세요.
pyo bo-yeo ju-se-yo.

위층으로 가세요.
wi-cheung-eu-ro ga-se-yo.

2층

1층

물품보관소가 어디예요?
mul-pum-bo-gwan-so-ga
eo-di-ye-yo?

바로 저기요.
ba-ro jeo-gi-yo.

아, 감사합니다.
a, gam-sa-ham-ni-da.

S: Your ticket, please.

S: Go upstairs. / M: Where is the coat check?

S: It's right there. / M: Ah, thanks.

Tip. Check coats and big bags at the theater!

Most theaters have coat checks and locker rooms for customer convenience. Check your belongings before entering the theater.

S2: Just one coat? / **M:** Yes.

S2: Here is your number.

M: Excuse me. This is my seat. / **A:** Oh? What's your seat number?

M: H7. / **A:** This one is G7.

M: Oh! So sorry. / **A:** No problem.

M: What is this line for? / P: The stadium entrance.

M: Where is the ticket counter? / P: On the opposite side.

M: Are you in line? / P2: Yes.

M: One adult. / C: Which section?

M: Any section is okay. Is there a front row seat?

C: Which side? /
M: The first base side. Seat in the cheering section, please.
C: No seats left. Only upper level seats are available.

M: How much is it? / C: Twenty thousand won.

M: Okay. I'll take one.

와, 사람이 너무 많아!
wa, sa-ra-mi neo-mu ma-na!

퀵패스가 있으면
빨리 탈 수 있어요.
kwik-pae-seu-ga i-sseu-myeon
bbal-ri tal ssu i-sseo-yo.

아, 한정판매라서 없대요.
a, han-jeong-pan-mae-ra-seo
eop-ddae-yo.

롤러코스터 타요.
rol-reo-ko-seu-teo ta-yo.

M: Wow, there are a lot of people! /
H: We could get on faster if we had Quick Passes.

H: Ah, they were sold out because of limited sales. /
M: Let's go on the roller coaster.

Tip. Quick Pass

If you get a Quick Pass (a special fast-pass for attractions), you don't have to queue to ride. Quick Passes are limited, however, so purchase in advance.

S: Put your belongings in the basket next to you.

S: Watch out! The safety bars are coming down.

Tip. Fantastic parades

Korean amusement parks like Lotte World in Seoul and Everland in Yongin are often good for a must-see parade. Don't miss them!

Useful words for booking online

- **티켓 구매** ti-ket gu-mae buy tickets

- **날짜** nal-jja date

- **시간** si-gan time

- **수량** su-ryang quantity

- **성인** seong-in adult /
  청소년 cheong-so-nyeon youth /
  어린이 eo-ri-ni child /
  우대 u-dae treatment (for senior or the disabled)

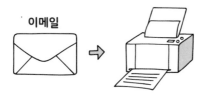

이메일

- **자리 선택** ja-ri seon-taek seat selection /
  선택한 좌석 seon-tae-kan jwa-seok selected seat

- **가능** ga-neung available

- **매진** mae-jin sold out

- **무대** mu-dae stage

- **줄** jul row

- **지금 예약** ji-geum ye-yak book now

- **취소** chwi-so cancel

- **삭제** sak-jje delete

- **결제** gyeol-jje payment

- **확인** hwa-gin review

- **확정** hwak-jjeong confirmation

6

Travel

여행 yeo-haeng

C: Hello. Your passport, please.

C: How many bags are you checking? / H: One.

C: Please put your bag here.

Tip. Check-in before leaving for the airport!

Check in via mobile phone or web in advance and avoid lining up at ticket counters. Simply check your baggage. Most distance check-ins are available 24 hours before departure and include seat selection.

C: Any batteries in your baggage? / **H:** No.

H: An aisle seat, please.
(A window seat) / **C:** Okay.

72번 탑승구에서 탑승하세요.
chil-si-bi-beon tap-sseung-gu-e-seo
tap-sseung-ha-se-yo.

탑승은 12시 20분에 시작합니다.
tap-sseung-eun yeol-ddu-si i-sip-bbu-ne si-ja-kam-ni-da.

12:20

늦어도 15분 전에는
탑승구에 가셔야 합니다.
neu-jeo-do si-bo-bun jeo-ne-neun
tap-sseung-gu-e ga-syeo-ya ham-ni-da.

12:05

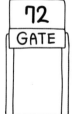

C: You can board at gate number 72.

C: Boarding begins at twelve-twenty.

C: You should get to the gate at least fifteen minutes before then.

+ **Extra Expressions** +

→ Checking your points & flight rewards

Did I get my travel points?

마일리지 적립됐어요?

ma-il-ri-ji jeong-nip-dwae-sseo-yo?

Am I entitled to points (flight rewards)?

마일리지를 받을 수 있어요?

ma-il-ri-ji-reul ba-deul ssu i-sseo-yo?

Can you tell me my point total?

마일리지가 총 얼마인지 알려 줄래요?

ma-il-ri-ji-ga chong eol-ma-in-ji al-ryeo jul-rae-yo?

→ When you check your baggage...

It's over the weight limit.

(짐이) 무게를 초과했어요.

(ji-mi) mu-ge-reul cho-gwa-hae-sseo-yo.

This will be a carry-on.

이것은 (기내에) 들고 타요.

i-geo-seun (gi-nae-e) deul-go ta-yo.

Could you put a 'fragile' label on it?

'파손 주의' 스티커를 붙여 주시겠어요?

'pa-son ju-i' seu-ti-keo-reul bu-cheo ju-si-ge-sseo-yo?

147

> 한국은 처음인가요?
> han-gu-geun cheo-eu-min-ga-yo?

> 네.
> ne.

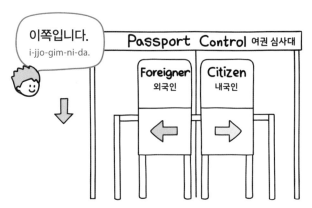

> 이쪽입니다.
> i-jjo-gim-ni-da.

Passport Control 여권 심사대

Foreigner	Citizen
외국인	내국인
←	→

S: Is this your first visit to Korea? /
H: Yes.

S: This way.

* 여권 심사대
yeo-ggwon sim-sa-dae
passport control
외국인 oe-gu-gin foreigner
내국인 nae-gu-gin citizen

I: What is the purpose of your visit? / H: Sightseeing. (business)

I: How long are you staying? / H: For one week.

I: Can I see your return ticket?

I: Will you be visiting anywhere else in Korea? /
H: Yes, Jeju-do and Yeosu.

I: Who are you traveling with? / H: By myself.

I: Look at the camera.

+ **Extra Expressions** +

→ Immigration FAQ

Have you ever been here?

이곳에 온 적 있습니까?

i-go-se on jeok it-sseum-ni-gga?

Are you traveling alone?

혼자 여행합니까?

hon-ja yeo-haeng-ham-ni-gga?

How long will you be staying?

얼마나 머무나요?

eol-ma-na meo-mu-na-yo?

Where will you be staying?

어디에 머무나요?

eo-di-e meo-mu-na-yo?

How much money do you have?

돈은 얼마나 가지고 있습니까?

do-neun eol-ma-na ga-ji-go it-sseum-ni-gga?

What's your occupation?

직업은 무엇입니까?

ji-geo-beun mu-eo-sim-ni-gga?

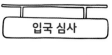

* 입국 심사 ip-gguk sim-sa immigration

C: Do you have anything to declare? / H: No.

C: Do you have any food? (alcohol / tobacco) / H: No.

➜ Customs Declaration FAQ

Show me your customs declaration card.

세관 신고서를 주세요.

se-gwan sin-go-seo-reul ju-se-yo.

Open this suitcase.

가방 열어 보세요.

ga-bang yeo-reo bo-se-yo.

What are these for?

이것들은 무슨 용도입니까?

i-geot-ddeu-reun mu-seun yong-do-im-ni-gga?

This item is not allowed.

이것은 반입 금지입니다.

i-geo-seun ba-nip geum-ji-im-ni-da.

You have to pay duty on this.

이것은 세금을 내야 합니다.

i-geo-seun se-geu-meul nae-ya ham-ni-da.

어떻게 환승해요?
eo-ddeo-ke hwan-seung-hae-yo?

'트랜스퍼' 사인을 따라가세요.
'teu-raen-seu-peo' sa-i-neul dda-ra-ga-se-yo.

환승
Transfer

실례합니다, 환승하려고 하는데요.
sil-rye-ham-ni-da, hwan-seung-ha-ryeo-go ha-neun-de-yo.

이 방향이 맞나요?
i bang-hyang-i man-na-yo?

네. 이쪽 줄로 가세요.
ne. i-jjok jjul-ro ga-se-yo.

입국 심사

H: How can I transfer? / **S:** Follow the 'Transfer' sign.

H: Excuse me, I want to transfer. Is this the right way? / **S2:** Yes. Get in this line.

* 환승
hwan-seung
transfer

154

몇 번 탑승구...?
아! 36번.
myeot bbeon tap-sseung-gu...?
a! sam-sim-nyuk-bbeon.

오, 이런,
비행기가 연착됐네.
o, i-reon, bi-haeng-gi-ga
yeon-chak-ddwaen-ne.

H: Which gate...? Ah! Number 36.

H: Oh, no, the flight is delayed.

* 출발 chul-bal **departure**

H: I'm really tired.

H: Excuse me, is this seat taken? / P: No.

A: Attention all Jeju Air passengers going to Jeju, we will soon begin boarding at gate 36.

➔ When the flight is delayed...

My flight was delayed.

비행기가 연착했어요.

bi-haeng-gi-ga yeon-cha-kae-sseo-yo.

Can I get a connecting flight?

연결 항공편을 탈 수 있을까요?

yeon-gyeol hang-gong-pyeo-neul tal ssu i-sseul-gga-yo?

How do I get to gate 11?

11번 탑승구는 어떻게 가요?

si-bil-beon tap-sseung-gu-neun eo-ddeo-ke ga-yo?

➔ When you miss the next flight...

I missed my flight.

비행기를 놓쳤어요.

bi-haeng-gi-reul not-cheo-sseo-yo.

When is the next flight?

다음 항공편은 언제 있나요?

da-eum hang-gong-pyeo-neun eon-je in-na-yo?

C: Your boarding pass, please.

C: Go this way.

H: One more blanket, please.

(pair of slippers / pair of earplugs / eye mask / toothbrush)

컵라면 먹을 수 있어요?

keom-na-myeon meo-geul ssu i-sseo-yo?

국내선은 안 됩니다. 죄송합니다.

gung-nae-seo-neun an doem-ni-da. joe-song-ham-ni-da.

비빔밥은요?

bi-bim-bba-beun-nyo?

사전에 주문하셔야 해요.

sa-jeo-ne ju-mun-ha-syeo-ya hae-yo.

그럼, 오렌지 주스 주세요.

geu-reom, o-ren-ji ju-seu ju-se-yo.

네.

ne.

H: Can I have a cup of noodles? /
C: We don't serve noodles on domestic flights. Sorry.

H: Can I order this bibimbap? / **C:** You have to order it in advance.

H: Then, orange juice please. / **C:** Yes.

H: Could you take this away, please?
H: Go ahead. / P: Thanks.

* 화장실 hwa-jang-sil lavatory
  비어 있음 bi-eo i-sseum vacant
  사용 중 sa-yong jung occupied

+ Extra Expressions +

➜ For a safe flight...

Please put your bag under your seat.

가방을 좌석 아래 두세요.

ga-bang-eul jwa-seok a-rae du-se-yo.

Please put your seat back upright.

좌석 등받이를 세워 주세요.

jwa-seok deung-ba-ji-reul se-wo ju-se-yo.

Please open your window shades.

창문 블라인드를 열어 주세요.

chang-mun beul-ra-in-deu-reul yeo-reo ju-se-yo.

The seat belt sign is on.

안전벨트 경고 등이 켜졌습니다.

an-jeon-bel-teu gyeong-go deung-i kyeo-jeot-sseum-ni-da.

➜ When you can't speak well in Korean...

Are there any English speakers?

영어 하는 분 계세요?

yeong-eo ha-neun bun gye-se-yo?

S: Hello! May I help you? /
H: Are there any city tours?

S: Today? / H: No, tomorrow.

* 관광안내소
gwan-gwang-an-ne-so
Tourist Information

162

S: A one-day tour? / H: Half-day.

H: How long is the tour? / S: Four hours.

H: When do they begin? / S: 8 a.m. or 2 p.m.

S: Which one do you prefer? / H: 2 p.m.

H: Can I book it here? / S: Yes.

H: Where is the meeting point? / S: In front of this center.

H: Nice!

S: Don't forget to bring this sheet.

H: Change your clothes and I'll meet you at the snack bar.

C: May I help you? /

M: Two bottles of sikhye and two hard-boiled eggs, please.

Tip. Korean's sauna culture

Koreans have a traditional floor-heating system called 'ondol,' which they enjoy in the colder months. A jjimjilbang is a public ondol sauna and a popular place to relax. Koreans also like to eat there; for example, sikye (a sweet-flavored traditional Korean beverage made with rice) and boiled egg.

H: So sweet and cool! / M: Fantastic!

H: Too hot! / M: I promise you'll feel refreshed. Enjoy it!

< Check-in >

체크인하려고요.
che-keu-in-ha-ryeo-go-yo.

신분증 주세요.
sin-bun-jjeung ju-se-yo.

하루 호텔

거의 다 됐습니다.
보증금을 위해 신용카드가 필요합니다.
geo-i da dwaet-sseum-ni-da. bo-jeung-geu-meul
wi-hae si-nyong-ka-deu-ga pi-ryo-ham-ni-da.

M: I'd like to check in, please. / **C:** May I have your ID?

C: Almost done. We also require a credit card for a damage deposit.

보증금이요?
bo-jeung-geu-mi-yo?

그냥 대기만 하고,
지금 청구하지 않습니다.
geu-nyang dae-gi-man ha-go, ji-geum
cheong-gu-ha-ji an-sseum-ni-da.

오전 7~10시

아침 식사는 오전
7시부터 10시까지입니다.
a-chim sik-ssa-neun o-jeon il-gop
ssi-bu-teo yeol ssi-gga-ji-im-ni-da.

하루 호텔
5층
4층
3층
2층
1층

식당은 1층에 있습니다.
sik-ddang-eun il-cheung-e
it-sseum-ni-da.

M: Damage deposit? /
C: We just swipe your card but don't
   charge it now.

C: Breakfast is from 7 to 10 a.m.

C: The restaurant is on the first floor.

Tip. **Deposit**

A credit card might be requested
when checking in. Usually
the hotel staff will swipe it
but not charge you anything
unless there is damage or an
unexpected loss of some kind.

169

수영장은 열려 있나요?
su-yeong-jang-eun yeol-ryeo in-na-yo?

네.
ne.

몇 시까지 열어요?
myeot ssi-gga-ji yeo-reo-yo?

저녁 9시요.
jeo-nyeok a-hop ssi-yo.

Tip. If you don't want to clean your room cleaned

If you want to rest until late in the morning, hang a '방해하지 마세요. (Do not disturb.)' sign on the doorknob.

M: Is the swimming pool open? / C: Yes.

M: How late is it open? / C: 9 p.m.

170

< Check-out >

체크아웃할게요.
che-keu-a-ut-hal-gge-yo.

청구서입니다.
cheong-gu-seo-im-ni-da.

하루 호텔

합계 :

이 요금은 뭐예요?
i yo-geu-meun mwo-ye-yo?

룸서비스 비용입니다.
rum-seo-bi-seu bi-yong-im-ni-da.

M: Check-out, please. / **C:** Here is the bill.

M: What is this charge? / **C:** It's for room service.

아, 알겠어요.
짐 좀 맡길 수 있어요?
a, al-ge-sseo-yo.
jim jom mat-ggil ssu i-sseo-yo?

그럼요. 언제 오세요?
geu-reom-nyo. eon-je o-se-yo?

3시쯤이요.
se si-jjeu-mi-yo.

하루 호텔

수하물표입니다.
su-hwa-mul-pyo-im-ni-da.

H34
996

H34
996

C: Ah, I see. Could you hold my baggage for a while?

C: Sure. When will you come back? / M: About 3 p.m.

C: Here's your baggage tag.

+ **Extra Expressions** +

➜ In the hotel lobby...

Do you have any vacancies?

빈방 있나요?

bin-bang in-na-yo?

Can I see the room first?

방 먼저 볼 수 있어요?

bang meon-jeo bol ssu i-sseo-yo?

Can I check in early?

조기 체크인 돼요?

jo-gi che-keu-in dwae-yo?

When is the check-out time?

체크아웃 시간이 언제예요?

che-keu-a-ut si-ga-ni eon-je-ye-yo?

Breakfast is included.

조식 포함입니다.

jo-sik po-ha-mim-ni-da.

➜ Useful words at the hotel

_모닝콜 mo-ning-kol **wake-up call**

_무료 제공 mu-ryo je-gong **complimentary**

_목욕 수건 mo-gyok su-geon **bath towel**

_더블룸 deo-beul-rum **double room**

_트윈룸 teu-win-rum **twin room**

Check! How to prepare for Korean travel!

• **Passport**: Prepare a copy of your passport ID page and some passport-sized color photos in the unfortunate event you lose your original. Depending on your country of origin, you may be able to get a temporary passport in a government office abroad. Also, for anyone planning to work in Korea, the photos will come in handy for certain registrations.
There are photo booths in various subway stations though.

• **Visa**: Citizens from several countries can visit Korea without a visa for travel under visa-waiver agreements of 30 to 180 days. Contact a Korean embassy or consulate in your country before visiting.

- **E-tickets**: Print out your e-ticket to keep track of your travel.

- **Local currency**: Bring Korean won and USD.

- **Credit cards / Debit cards**: Verify that they can be used overseas.

- **SIM cards**: Order in advance or buy one in Korea.

- **Booking vouchers**: Print out any vouchers for hotels, tours, and performances.

- **220V adapter**: The C and F plug type is used in Korea. The electrical supply is 220V at 60Hz.

- **Useful apps**: Download apps for maps, taxis, translation and other conveniences.

- **Others**: Travel insurance, international driver's license, international student cards and discount coupons.

7

Daily Life & Emergencies
일상 & 응급 il-ssang & eung-geup

< **At a convenience store** >

저기요.
맥주 어디 있어요?
jeo-gi-yo.
maek-jju eo-di i-sseo-yo?

뒤쪽 냉장고에 있습니다.
dwi-jjok naeng-jang-go-e
it-sseum-ni-da.

어느 쪽이요?
eo-neu jjo-gi-yo?

맨 왼쪽이요.
maen oen-jjo-gi-yo.

오른쪽 o-reun-jjok

M: Excuse me. Where is the beer? /
C: They are in the refrigerator, at the back of the store.

M: Which side? / **C:** The far left side. (right side)

178

M: Could you give me change for a 1,000 bill? (5,000 / 10,000) /
C: Oops! We don't have enough.

M: That's okay then.

< **At a supermarket** >

과일이 별론데!
gwa-i-ri byeol-ron-de!

와! 빵이다!
wa! bbang-i-da!

계란 gye-ran /
치즈 chi-jeu /
우유 u-yu

1+1이네.
won-peul-reo-seu-wo-ni-ne.

H: This fruit doesn't look good!

H: Wow! Bread! (eggs / cheese / milk)

H: Buy one, get one free.

Tip. 계란? 달걀?
"계란" and "달걀" mean "egg"
in Korean.

C: Membership card? / H: No.

H: You charged me twice for this. / C: Oh! I'm so sorry. I'll cancel it.

+ **Extra Expressions** +

➜ At a grocery stores...

I can't see the best-before date.

유효 기간을 못 찾겠어요.

yu-hyo gi-ga-neul mot chat-gge-sseo-yo.

Could I taste this?

이거 시식할 수 있어요?

i-geo si-si-kal ssu i-sseo-yo?

Could you vacuum-pack it?

진공 포장 돼요?

jin-gong po-jang dwae-yo?

Do you have a smaller one?

더 작은 거 있어요?

deo ja-geun geo i-sseo-yo?

Please wrap it so it won't melt.

녹지 않게 포장해 주세요.

nok-jji an-ke po-jang-hae ju-se-yo.

➜ At a convenience store...

One more <u>chopsticks</u>, please.

<u>젓가락</u> 하나 더 주세요.

jeot-gga-rak ha-na deo ju-se-yo.

_숟가락 sut-gga-rak **spoon**

_포크 po-keu **fork**

_빨대 bbal-ddae **straw**

Do you have a fork?

포크 있어요?

po-keu i-sseo-yo?

Could you tell me where the hot water is?

뜨거운 물 어디 있어요?

ddeu-geo-un mul eo-di i-sseo-yo?

Could you tell me where I throw away the (ramen) soup?

(라면) 국물 어디에 버려요?

(ra-myeon) gung-mul eo-di-e beo-ryeo-yo?

➜ At the counter...

You gave me a 1,000 won less.

천 원 덜 거슬러 줬어요.

cheon won deol geo-seul-reo jwo-sseo-yo.

One more <u>plastic / paper</u> bag, please.

<u>비닐 / 종이</u> 봉투 하나 더 주세요.

bi-nil / jong-i bong-tu ha-na deo ju-se-yo.

Wrap these separately, please.

따로 포장해 주세요.

dda-ro po-jang-hae ju-se-yo.

< **How to use an ATM** >

1. **언어 선택** eo-neo seon-taek (**영어** yeong-eo)

→ 2. **카드 선택** ka-deu seon-taek (**해외 발급** hae-oe bal-geup)

→ 3. **거래 선택** geo-rae seon-taek (**출금** chul-geum)

→ 4. **카드 삽입** ka-deu sa-bip

→ 5. **비밀번호 입력** bi-mil-beon-ho im-nyeok
   출금액 선택 chul-geu-maek seon-taek
   원하는 출금액 입력 won-ha-neun chul-geu-maek im-nyeok

→ 6. **명세표를 원하십니까?** myeong-se-pyo-reul won-ha-sim-ni-gga?
   (**예** ye / **아니요** a-ni-yo)

진행 중... jin-haeng jung

죄송하지만, 거래가 거절되었습니다.
joe-song-ha-ji-man, geo-rae-ga geo-jeol-doe-eot-sseum-ni-da.

잔액을 확인하세요. ja-nae-geul hwa-gin-ha-se-yo.

1. Select a language (English)
2. Select for a card issued overseas or in Korea (issued overseas)
3. Select a transaction (withdrawal)
4. Insert card
5. Enter your PIN
   Enter the amount of your withdrawal
   Choose an amount
6. Would you like a receipt? (Yes / No)

Processing...
Sorry, your transaction is denied.
Check your balance.

H: What's wrong? It won't accept my card.

H: Let's try another machine.

H: Thank goodness!

P: How can I help you? / H: I'm here to make a report.

P: Can you explain what happened? / H: I can't speak Korean.

H: Any English speakers? /
P: No.

H: Please call the embassy.

Tip. **When you go to the police station...**

If it's hard to explain the situation accurately in Korean, ask them to contact an interpreter or your embassy.

+ Extra Expressions +

➡ When you ask someone to call the police...

Call the police, please.

경찰에 신고해 주세요.

gyeong-cha-re sin-go-hae ju-se-yo.

➡ When you need help from an interpreter or embassy...

I lost my passport.

여권을 잃어버렸어요.

yeo-ggwo-neul i-reo-beo-ryeo-sseo-yo.

Please call the U.S. embassy.

미국 대사관에 연락해 주세요.

mi-guk dae-sa-gwa-ne yeol-ra-kae ju-se-yo.

_영국 yeong-guk British

_호주 ho-ju Australian

An English interpreter, please.

영어 통역사 좀 불러 주세요.

yeong-eo tong-yeok-ssa jom bul-reo ju-se-yo.

➡ When you want to use the telephone...

I want to make a phone call.

전화하고 싶어요.

jeon-hwa-ha-go si-peo-yo.

➡ When you want to report a crime...

I'm here to report <u>an assault</u>.

폭행 신고하러 왔어요.

po-kaeng sin-go-ha-reo wa-sseo-yo.

_강도 gang-do a robbery
_절도 jeol-ddo a theft
_날치기 nal-chi-gi a snatching
_소매치기 so-mae-chi-gi a pickpocket
_교통사고 gyo-tong-sa-go a car accident
_빵소니 사고 bbaeng-so-ni sa-go a hit-and-run

Someone took my bag.

누가 내 가방을 가져갔어요.

nu-ga nae ga-bang-eul ga-jeo-ga-sseo-yo.

M: Can I see a doctor right now? It's an emergency.

N: Please fill out this form first.

< **Medical background** >

1. **나이** na-i age

2. **혈액형** hyeo-rae-kyeong blood type

3. **병력** byeong-ryeok chronic illness
   _**고혈압** go-hyeo-rap high blood pressure
   _**당뇨** dang-nyo diabetes
   _**천식** cheon-sik asthma
   _**심장병** sim-jang-bbyeong heart disease
   _**기타** gi-ta etc.

4. **여성인 경우만** yeo-seong-in gyeong-u-man for women only
   임신 중 im-sin jung (**예** ye / **아니요** a-ni-yo) pregnant (Yes / No)

5. **복용하는 약이 있습니까?** (**예** ye / **아니요** a-ni-yo)
   bo-gyong-ha-neun ya-gi it-sseum-ni-gga?

   Do you take any medication? (Yes / No)

   '예'를 선택했으면, 여기에 상세한 내용을 적으세요.
   'ye'-reul seon-tae-kae-sseu-myeon, yeo-gi-e sang-se-han nae-yong-eul jeo-geu-se-yo.

   If you selected 'yes,' provide details here.

괜찮아요?
gwaen-cha-na-yo?

아니요, 어지러워요.
a-ni-yo, eo-ji-reo-wo-yo.

열 있어요?
yeol i-sseo-yo?

네. 독감 걸린 거 같아요.
ne. dok-ggam geol-rin geo ga-ta-yo.

M: Are you okay? / **H:** No, I feel dizzy.

M: Do you have a fever? / **H:** Yes. I think I have the flu.

M: Since when? / H: Yesterday. / M: Let's go to the pharmacy.

P: Hello. How are you feeling? /

H: I have a little headache. (a slight fever)

P: Take this, three times a day.

M: Get some rest! / H: I see, thanks.

+ **Extra Expressions** +

➜ Useful words for hospitals

_땀 ddam sweat

_기침 gi-chim cough

_한기 | han-gi chill

_구토 gu-to vomiting

_설사 seol-ssa diarrhea

_발진 bal-jjin rash

_피 | pi blood

_멍 meong bruise

_상처 sang-cheo, 흉터 hyung-teo scar

_혈압 hyeo-rap blood pressure

_마비 ma-bi paralysis

_수술 su-sul operation

_주사 ju-sa injection

➜ Useful words for phamacies

_진통제 jin-tong-je pain killer

_(가려움 방지) 연고 (ga-ryeo-um bang-ji) yeon-go anti-itch cream

_해열제 hae-yeol-jje fever reducer

_소화제 so-hwa-je digestive aid

_감기약 gam-gi-yak cold relief

_알레르기 약 al-re-reu-gi yak allergy relief

_반창고 ban-chang-go Band-Aid

_멀미 약 meol-mi yak motion sickness medicine

_고산병 약 go-san-bbyeong yak altitude medicine

_처방전 cheo-bang-jeon prescription

→ At hospital reception

Do you take walk-ins?

예약 안 해도 돼요?

ye-yak an hae-do dwae-yo?

Do you have health insurance?

건강보험에 가입되었어요?

geon-gang-bo-heo-me ga-ip-ddoe-eo-sseo-yo?

→ Explaining your symtoms

I don't know how to explain my symptoms in Korean.

한국어로 증상을 말하기 어려워요.

han-gu-geo-ro jeung-sang-eul mal-ha-gi eo-ryeo-wo-yo.

My <u>stomach</u> is killing me.

배가 너무 아파요.

bae-ga neo-mu a-pa-yo.

_눈 nun eye(s)

_코 ko nose

_귀 gwi ear(s)

_목 mok throat

_이 i tooth/teeth

_다리 da-ri leg(s)

<u>Slight / Severe</u> pain.

통증이 약해요 / 심해요.

tong-jjeung-i ya-kae-yo / sim-hae-yo.

→ About dosage and efficacy

How do I take this?

이거 어떻게 복용해요?
i-geo eo-ddeo-ke bo-gyong-hae-yo?

Will I get drowsy (if I take this)?

(이거 먹으면) 졸리나요?
(i-geo meo-geu-myeon) jol-ri-na-yo?

Any side effects?

부작용 있나요?
bu-ja-gyong in-na-yo?

After meals.

식후에 드세요. (빈속에 먹지 마세요.)
si-ku-e deu-se-yo. (bin-so-ge meok-jji ma-se-yo.)

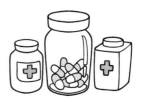

Enjoy the Korean holidays!

1. Seollal (설날)

Seollal (Lunar New Year's Day) is Korea's most important traditional seasonal festival. It occurs on the first day of the lunar calendar but includes both the day before and after. Koreans during this time will return home in waves to celebrate the occasion. Eating tteokguk (rice cake soup) signifies becoming one year older. If someone eats two bowls, the joke is that that person just got two years older. Also on this day, young people bow to their elders (called "sebae") after which the elders present New Year's gifts of money to their juniors.

2. Daeboreum (대보름)

Daeboreum (Great Full Moon) celebrates the first full moon of the lunar calendar. On that day, people eat a special festival food called ogokbap (a dish made with five grains) and say "Buy my heat!" to each other as a playful way to avoid the heat of the coming summer season.

3. Chuseok (추석)

Chuseok is held on the fifteenth day of August by the lunar calendar (September to early October by the solar calendar) and is similar to Thanksgiving Day. During Chuseok, family members gather together with newly harvested crops to give thanks to their ancestors and to nature. While enjoying the harvest moon that evening, they send forth personal prayers and hopes. Among the day's special foods is songpyeon, a kind of rice cake steamed with the help of pine needles. "Song" means pine tree.

4. Christmas (크리스마스)

Most Koreans, including the near 30% population of Christians, look forward to Christmas. They exchange gifts and cards, buy specially decorated cakes and decorate trees. They might even get a day off, as the 25th is a public holiday. Don't expect stuffed turkey dinners or children queuing to see Santa though. Certain aspects of the holiday have not translated.

8

Basic Expressions

기본 표현 gi-bon pyo-hyeon

안녕하세요! 잘 지내요?
an-nyeong-ha-se-yo! jal ji-nae-yo?

잘 지내요, 당신은요?
jal ji-nae-yo, dang-si-neun-nyo?

저도 잘 지내요.
jeo-do jal ji-nae-yo.

H: Hi! How are you?

M: I'm good, and you? /

H: I'm fine, too.

Tip. 식사했어요? sik-ssa-hae-sseo-yo?
Korean often say each other, "식사했어요? (Did you have a meal yet?)" to each other. This isn't to see if you've eaten though, just to ask how you are.

H: Goodbye! / M: See you!
H: Take care! / M: Let's keep in touch.

M: I'm Michael. May I have your name? / H: I'm Heather.

M: Where are you from? / H: I'm from America.

H: What do you do for a living? / M: I'm an engineer. How about you?

H: I'm a student. (an office worker)

H: Thank you! / M: You're welcome.

H: Thanks a lot! / M: No problem.

M: Thank you so much! / H: My pleasure.

H: You're so kind. / M: It's my pleasure.

늦었네요. 죄송합니다.
neu-jeon-ne-yo. joe-song-ham-ni-da.

괜찮습니다.
gwaen-chan-sseum-ni-da.

그건 정말 미안합니다.
geu-geon jeong-mal mi-an-ham-ni-da.

H: I'm late. I'm sorry. / M: That's alright.

H: I'm so sorry about that.

M: I apologize. / H: It's not a big deal.
M: It was my fault. / H: Don't worry.

H: Excuse me. / M: Just a moment.

M: What's up? / H: Help me, please!

M: Would you do me a favor? / H: Of course.

M: Pardon me, please? / H: Okay.

M: I'll go to Korea. / **H:** Pardon?

M: I said I'll go to Korea. / **H:** Ah, good for you.

H: Anyway, really? / M: Yes.

H: You're kidding me. / M: No. I'm serious.

H: Wow! Have a nice trip!

M: Yes! / H: Amazing! /

M: Awesome! / H: Perfect! /

M: Good!

Tip. If you add '-요 yo,' to an expression it becomes more polite.

M: No! / **H:** Oh my god! / **M:** Terrible! / **H:** Be quiet!

[Numbers 숫자]

one	two	three	four	five
1 / 하나	2 / 둘	3 / 셋	4 / 넷	5 / 다섯
il / ha-na	i / dul	sam / set	sa / net	o / da-seot

six	seven	eight	nine	ten
6 / 여섯	7 / 일곱	8 / 여덟	9 / 아홉	10 / 열
yuk / yeo-seot	chil / il-gop	pal / yeo-deol	gu / a-hop	sip / yeol

eleven	twelve	thirteen
11 / 열하나	12 / 열둘	13 / 열셋
si-bil / yeol-ha-na	si-bi / yeol-ddul	sip-ssam / yeol-set

fourteen	fifteen	twenty
14 / 열넷	15 / 열다섯	20 / 스물
sip-ssa / yeol-net	si-bo / yeol-da-seot	i-sip / seu-mul

thirty	forty	fifty
30 / 서른	40 / 마흔	50 / 쉰
sam-sip / seo-reun	sa-sip / ma-heun	o-sip / swin

sixty	seventy	eighty
60 / 예순	70 / 일흔	80 / 여든
yuk-ssip / ye-sun	chil-ssip / il-heun	pal-ssip / yeo-deun

ninety	hundred	thousand
90 / 아흔	100 / 백	1,000 / 천
gu-sip / a-heun	baek	cheon

[Money 화폐]
Korean money: 원 won

· bill, note: **지폐** ji-pye/ji-pe

one thousand won	five thousand won
1,000원 / 천 원 cheon won	5,000원 / 오천 원 o-cheon won
ten thousand won	fifty thousand won
10,000원 / 만 원 man won	50,000원 / 오만 원 o-man won

· coin: **동전** dong-jeon

a won	five won
1원 / 일 원 il won	5원 / 오 원 o won
ten won	fifty won
10원 / 십 원 sip won	50원 / 오십 원 o-sip won
one hundred won	five hundred won
100원 / 백 원 baek won	500원 / 오백 원 o-baek won

Tip. Given inflation over the years, '1원' and '5원' are not used in daily life. And these days, '10원' is rarely used either.

· check, cheque: **수표** su-pyo

Tip. In Korea, they use checks for more than a hundred thousand won.

[Dates 날짜]

Sunday	Monday	Tuesday	Wednesday
일요일	월요일	화요일	수요일
i-ryo-il	wo-ryo-il	hwa-yo-il	su-yo-il

	Thursday	Friday	Saturday
	목요일	금요일	토요일
	mo-gyo-il	gcu-myo-il	to-yo-il

Tip. In Korea, the week begins on Monday.

January	February	March	April
1월 / 일월	2월 / 이월	3월 / 삼월	4월 / 사월
i-rwol	i-wol	sa-mwol	sa-wol

May	June	July	August
5월 / 오월	6월 / 유월	7월 / 칠월	8월 / 팔월
o-wol	yu-wol	chi-rwol	pa-rwol

September	October	November	December
9월 / 구월	10월 / 시월	11월 / 십일월	12월 / 십이월
gu-wol	si-wol	si-bi-rwol	si-bi-wol

Tip. '6월' and '10월' are pronounced as "yu-wol" and "si-wol," not "yu-gwol" and "si-bwol." These are some of the exceptions that are used as opposed to the original pronunciation.

[**Time** 시간]

What time is it?

몇 시예요?

myeot ssi-ye-yo?

2:00

두 시예요.
2시예요.

du si-ye-yo.

2:10

두 시 십 분이에요.
2시 10분이에요.

du si sip bbu-ni-e-yo.

2:30 / It's half past two.

두 시 삼십 분이에요. / 두 시 반이에요.
2시 30분이에요. / 2시 반이에요.

du si sam-sip bbu-ni-e-yo. / du si ba-ni-e-yo.

2:50 / It's ten to three.

두 시 오십 분이에요. / 세 시 십 분 전이에요.
2시 50분이에요. / 3시 10분 전이에요.

du si o-sip bbu-ni-e-yo. / se si sip bbun jeo-ni-e-yo.

Review

01 # At a Café 카페에서 p.16

H: 카페라테 주세요.

C: 어떤 사이즈요? / H: 작은 거요.

C: 다른 건요? / H: 됐어요.

C: 여기서 드실 거예요? / H: 아니요, 가져갈 거예요.

C: 진동 벨이 울리면 오세요. / H: 네.

02 # Ordering Brunch 브런치 주문하기 p.20

H: 한 명이요. / W: 이쪽으로 오세요.

W: 주문하시겠어요? / H: 아직이요.

H: 저기요! / H: 이거요.

W: 음료는요? / H: 됐어요.

W: 음식 나왔습니다. / H: 감사합니다.

W: 다 괜찮으세요? / H: 네.

W: 다 드셨어요? / H: 네.

W: 더 필요하신 건요? / H: 없어요. 계산서 주세요.

03 # At a Snack Bar 분식집에서 p.26

H: 메뉴가 정말 많은데!

H: 치즈김밥 하나, 떡라면 하나요. / C: 선불입니다. 8천 원입니다.

C: 거스름돈 2천 원이요. / H: 감사합니다.

C: 맛있게 드세요.

04 # At a BBQ Restaurant 고깃집에서 p.28

M: 여기, 삼겹살 2인분 주세요.

M: 반찬 더 주세요. / H: 상추도요!

M: 양념갈비 2인분 주세요. / C: 네.

C: 불판 바꿔 드릴게요.

M: 냉면 먹을래요? / H: 배 안 불러요?

M: 고기 다음엔 냉면이래요. / H: 한번 먹어 볼까?

07 # Ordering Beer & Cocktails 맥주 & 칵테일 주문하기 p.42

M: 맥주 있어요? / B: 네.

B: 생맥주요, 병맥주요? / M: 생맥주 주세요.

H: 칵테일 뭐 있어요? / B: 여기 리스트 있어요.

H: 모히토 주세요. / B: 네.

M & H: 건배!

H: 내가 낼게요. / M: 아니에요.

M: 내가 쏠게요. / H: 고마워요!

08 # Ordering Food Delivery 배달 음식 주문하기 p.46

C: 하루반점입니다. /

M: 짜장면 하나, 짬뽕 하나, 탕수육 작은 거 하나요.

C: 2만 5천 원입니다. 어떻게 결제하실 거예요? / M: 현금이요.

C: 주소는요? / M: 화평로 15, 204호예요.

- 음식 배달 앱 설치 실행
- 위치 설정 (예. 마포구 합정동)
- 음식 카테고리 / 음식 선택 / 음식점 선택
- 메뉴 선택 / 추가 주문 (음료수 등)
- 가격 / 수량 – 주문하기
- 주소 / 휴대폰 번호 – 요청 사항 메모
- 결제 방법 선택
  - 현장 결제 : 신용카드 / 현금
  - 앱 결제 : 신용카드 / 현금 / 계좌 이체
- 주문 완료

W: 예약하셨어요? / H: 아니요.

W: 지금 자리가 없어요.

H: 대기자 명단에 올려 주세요.

W: 야외요 실내요? / H: 야외요.

H: 얼마나 기다려야 해요? / W: 15분 정도요.

10 # Buying a SIM Card 유심 사기

p.58

M: 유심 있어요? / C: 네. 어떤 요금제요?

M: 데이터 무제한 있어요? /

C: 이거 어떠세요? 데이터, 통화, 문자 무제한이에요.

M: 얼마예요? / C: 7만 7천 원이요.

M: 이걸로 할게요. / C: 네. 신분증 주세요.

11 # Using Wi-Fi 와이파이 사용하기

p.60

H: 무료 와이파이 있어요? / C: 네.

H: 어느 거예요? / C: CAFE-FREE입니다.

H: 비밀번호는요? / C: 영수증에 있어요.

H: 된다!

H: 사진 업로드 해 볼까?

H: 오, 빠른데.

H: 어? 갑자기 연결이 끊겼어.

12 # Doing Social Networking SNS 하기

p.64

H: 페이스북 해요? / M: 네.

M: 내 사진들을 올려요. / H: 오, 좋네요.

H: 친구 추가해 줘요.

M: 페이스북 이름이 뭐예요? / H: 헤더 브라운이에요.

M: 친구 찾기 해 볼게요.

M: 이게 당신이에요? / H: 네, 저예요.

M: 친구 요청 보냈어요. / H: 알았어요.

H: 추가할게요. / M: 좋아요! 연락하고 지내요.

13 # Taking Pictures 사진 찍기

p.68

H: 저기요. 사진 좀 찍어 주실래요? / P: 물론이죠.

H: 배경 나오게요. / P: 네.

H: 사진이 흐려요.

H: 한 장 더 부탁해요. / P: 네.

H: 정말 감사합니다.

14 # Making a Phone Call 전화 통화하기 p.72

M: 여보세요. 누구세요? / H: 헤더예요.

M: 오! 이거 당신 번호예요? / H: 네, 번호 바꿨어요.

15 # Borrowing a Charger 충전기 빌리기 p.74

H: 내 배터리가 다 됐어요.

H: 충전기 있어요? / M: 네.

H: 콘센트 어디 있어요? / M: 저기요.

M: 부재중 세 통이네. 지금 가야 해요.

H: 이거 어떻게 돌려주죠? / M: 문자해요.

18 # At a Shoe Shop 신발 가게에서 p.84

S: 뭘 찾으세요? / M: 운동화요.

S: 이거 어떠세요? / M: 오! 마음에 들어요.

M: 260 신어 볼 수 있어요? / S: 죄송하지만, 그 사이즈는 없어요.

S: 265 신어 보실래요?

M: 맞아요.

19 # At a Cosmetics Store 화장품 가게에서 p.86

H: 스킨 찾고 있는데요.

H: 뭐가 잘 나가요? / S: 이거요.

H: 지성 피부에 괜찮아요? / S: 네, 모든 피부용이에요.

H: 써 봐도 돼요? / S: 네, 이 테스터 써 보세요.

S: 마음에 드세요? / H: 약간 끈적이는데요.

20 # Payment & Tax Refunds 계산 & 세금 환급 p.90

C: 총 4만 5천 원입니다.

H: 할인 가격인가요? / C: 네.

H: 세금 환급하고 싶은데요. / C: 여권 주세요.

C: 상품과 부가세 환급증 잘 챙기세요.

H: 카드로 할게요. / C: 서명해 주세요.

C: 여기 영수증이요.

21 # Refunds & Exchanges 환불 & 교환 p.94

M: 환불하고 싶어요.

C: 영수증 있으세요? / M: 네, 여기요.

C: 할인 상품이었군요.

C: 죄송하지만, 환불이 안 돼요.

M: 근데, 여기 흠이 있어요. / C: 음...

M: 교환할 수 있어요?

C: 네, 다른 상품으로 가져오세요. / M: 고마워요.

22 # Online Shopping Service 온라인 쇼핑 서비스 p.98

안녕하세요.

제 이름은 헤더이고, 주문 번호는 12345입니다.

파손된 상품을 받았습니다.

반품하고 환불 받으려고요.

사진을 첨부합니다.

확인 후 다음 절차를 알려 주시기 바랍니다.

답장 기다리겠습니다.

안녕히 계세요.

헤더 드림

23 # Taking the Bus & Metro 버스 & 지하철 타기 p.104

H: 버스 정류장이 어디예요? / P: 여기서 두 블록 가세요.

H: 이 방향이요? / P: 네.

H: 거기서 시내 가는 버스를 탈 수 있어요? /

P: 아니요. 갈아타야 해요.

H: 가장 좋은 방법은 뭐예요? / P: 지하철이요.

H: 지하철역은 어떻게 가요? / P: 가장 가까운 역은...

P: 바로 저 모퉁이예요.

H: 명동 가는 표 한 장이요.

H: 명동 가는 방향이 어느 쪽이죠? / P2: 반대편이요.

24 # Taking a Taxi 택시 타기

D: 어디로 모실까요? / M: 시청까지 부탁합니다.

D: 안전벨트 매 주세요.

M: 길이 막히네!

M: 얼마나 걸려요? / D: 20분 정도요.

M: 여기 세워 주세요.

M: 잔돈 가지세요.

25 # Riding a Train 기차 타기

- 예약
- 패스 종류 / 출발일
- 개인 정보
- 결제
- 내 예약
  - 날짜 선택
  - 좌석 예약 / 좌석 선택
- 예약 완료

H: 좌석 예약했죠? / M: 어? 코레일 패스로 그냥 타는 거 아니에요?

H: 아니요, 예약해야 해요. 안 했으면, 역에서 하면 돼요.

M: 부산행 좌석 예약하려고요. / T: 코레일 패스와 여권 보여 주세요.

M: 감사합니다.

26 # Using Rental Cars 렌터카 이용하기 p.114

M: 인터넷으로 예약했어요. 여기 예약 확인서요.

S: 신분증과 운전면허증 주세요.

S: 내용 확인해 주세요.

M: 자동 변속기, 휘발유, 내비게이션, 종합 보험. 자차 손해 면책
제도는요?

S: '고객 부담금 면제, 5만 원 또는 30만 원 부담'이 있어요. /

M: '면제'로 해 주세요.

S: 차는 주차장에 있습니다. 따라오세요.

S: 차를 확인하시고, 여기에 서명해 주세요.

27 # At a Gas Station 주유소에서 p.120

H: 휘발유, 5만 원이요. / S: 결제해 드리겠습니다.

S: 창문을 닦아 드릴까요? / H: 네, 부탁합니다.

S: 주유 완료되었습니다. 안전 운전하세요.

시작 버튼 클릭

→ 유종 체크 (고급 휘발유 / 무연 휘발유 / 경유)

→ 금액 또는 주유량 체크

→ 결제

→ 주유기 삽입

→ 주유 시작

→ 영수증

28 # Museums & Art Galleries 박물관 & 미술관 p.126

G: 가방 열어 주세요.

H: 성인 한 장이요. 오디오 가이드도요.

H: 얼마예요? / C: 오디오 가이드는 무료입니다.

C: 오디오 가이드는 2층에서 가져가시면 됩니다. / H: 감사합니다.

S: 미국 사람인가요? / H: 네.

S: 영어로 드릴까요? / H: 영어랑 한국어 주세요.

S: 신분증 주세요.

29 # Theaters 공연장 p.130

M: 오늘 밤 이 공연 하나요? / S: 네.

M: 지금 들어갈 수 있어요? / S: 아직이요. 10분 후에 오세요.

S: 표 보여 주세요.

S: 위층으로 가세요. / M: 물품보관소가 어디예요?

S: 바로 저기요. / M: 아, 감사합니다.

S2: 코트 하나요? / M: 네.

S2: 여기 번호표요.

M: 실례합니다. 여기 제 자리인데요. / A: 그래요? 좌석 번호가 뭐예요?

M: H7이요. / A: 여기는 G7이에요.

M: 아! 죄송합니다. / A: 괜찮습니다.

30 # Stadiums 경기장 p.134

M: 이 줄은 뭐예요? / P: 경기장 입장하는 거요.

M: 매표소는 어디예요? / P: 반대쪽이요.

M: 줄 서신 거예요? / P2: 네.

M: 성인 한 장이요. / C: 어느 구역이요?

M: 아무데나요. 앞쪽 자리 있어요?

C: 어느 쪽이요? / M: 1루 쪽이요. 응원석으로요.

C: 남은 자리가 없어요. 위층 자리만 가능해요.

M: 얼마예요? / C: 2만 원입니다.

M: 네. 그걸로 할게요.

31 # Amusement Parks 놀이동산 p.138

M: 와, 사람이 너무 많아! / H: 퀵패스가 있으면 빨리 탈 수 있어요.

H: 아, 한정판매라서 없대요. / M: 롤러코스터 타요.

S: 휴대품은 옆 바구니에 넣으세요.

S: 조심하세요! 안전바 내립니다.

32 # Airports & Baggage 공항 & 수하물 p.144

C: 안녕하세요. 여권 주세요.

C: 부칠 짐은 몇 개예요? / H: 한 개요.

C: 가방 여기 올려 주세요.

C: 짐 안에 배터리 있어요? / H: 아니요.

H: 통로석으로 주세요. / C: 네.

C: 72번 탑승구에서 탑승하세요.

C: 탑승은 12시 20분에 시작합니다.

C: 늦어도 15분 전에는 탑승구에 가셔야 합니다.

33 # Immigration 입국 심사 p.148

S: 한국은 처음인가요? / H: 네.

S: 이쪽입니다.

I: 방문 목적은요? / H: 여행입니다.

I: 얼마나 체류해요? / H: 일주일이요.

I: 귀국 항공권을 보여 주세요.

I: 한국에서 다른 도시도 가세요? / H: 네, 제주도와 여수요.

I: 일행은요? / H: 혼자요.

I: 카메라 보세요.

34 # Customs Declaration 세관 신고 p.152

C: 신고할 게 있습니까? / H: 아니요.

C: 음식물 있어요? / H: 아니요.

35 # Transfers 환승 p.154

H: 어떻게 환승해요? / S: '트랜스퍼' 사인을 따라가세요.

H: 실례합니다, 환승하려고 하는데요. 이 방향이 맞나요? /

S2: 네. 이쪽 줄로 가세요.

H: 몇 번 탑승구...? 아! 36번.

H: 오, 이런, 비행기가 연착됐네.

H: 진짜 피곤하다.

H: 저기요, 여기 자리 있나요? / P: 아니요.

A: 제주로 가는 제주 항공 승객들께 알려 드립니다. 36번 탑승구에서 탑승을 시작합니다.

36 # On an Airplane 기내에서 p.158

C: 탑승권 주세요.

C: 이쪽으로 가세요.

H: 담요 하나 더 주세요.

H: 컵라면 먹을 수 있어요? / C: 국내선은 안 됩니다. 죄송합니다.

H: 비빔밥은요? / C: 사전에 주문하셔야 해요.

H: 그럼, 오렌지 주스 주세요. / C: 네.

H: 이거 치워 주시겠어요?

H: 먼저 가세요. / P: 고마워요.

37 # Local Touring 지역 관광 p.162

S: 안녕하세요! 뭘 도와드릴까요? / H: 시티 투어 있어요?

S: 오늘이요? / H: 아니요, 내일이요.

S: 종일 투어요? / H: 반일이요.

H: 몇 시간짜리예요? / S: 4시간이요.

H: 언제 시작해요? / S: 오전 8시, 오후 2시 있어요.

S: 어느 게 더 좋으세요? / H: 오후 2시요.

H: 여기서 예약하나요? / S: 네.

H: 만나는 곳은 어디예요? / S: 이 센터 앞이요.

H: 좋네요!

S: 이 종이 꼭 가져오세요.

38 # At a Jjimjilbang 찜질방에서 p.166

H: 옷 갈아입고 매점 앞에서 만나요.

C: 뭘 드릴까요? / M: 식혜와 삶은 달걀 두 개 주세요.

H: 달콤하고 시원해요! / M: 환상적이죠!

H: 너무 뜨거워요! / M: 피로가 풀려요. 즐겨 봐요!

39 # Accommodations 숙소 p.168

M: 체크인하려고요. / C: 신분증 주세요.

C: 거의 다 됐습니다. 보증금을 위해 신용카드가 필요합니다.

M: 보증금이요? / C: 그냥 대기만 하고, 지금 청구하지 않습니다.

C: 아침 식사는 오전 7시부터 10시까지입니다.

C: 식당은 1층에 있습니다.

M: 수영장은 열려 있나요? / C: 네.

M: 몇 시까지 열어요? / C: 저녁 9시요.

M: 체크아웃할게요. / C: 청구서입니다.

M: 이 요금은 뭐예요? / C: 룸서비스 비용입니다.

M: 아, 알겠어요. 짐 좀 맡길 수 있어요?

C: 그럼요. 언제 오세요? / M: 3시쯤이요.

C: 수하물표입니다.

M: 저기요. 맥주 어디 있어요? / C: 뒤쪽 냉장고에 있습니다.

M: 어느 쪽이요? / C: 맨 왼쪽이요.

M: 천 원짜리로 거슬러 주실 수 있어요? / C: 앗! 부족할 거 같은데요.

M: 그럼 괜찮습니다.

H: 과일이 별론데!

H: 와! 빵이다!

H: 1+1이네.

C: 회원카드 있으세요? / H: 없어요.

H: 이거 중복 계산했어요. / C: 오! 죄송합니다. 취소해 드릴게요.

41 # Using a Cash Machine 현금자동지급기 사용하기 p.184

1. 언어 선택 (영어)

2. 카드 선택 (해외 발급)

3. 거래 선택 (출금)

4. 카드 삽입

5. 비밀번호 입력

   출금액 선택

   원하는 출금액 입력

6. 명세표를 원하십니까? (예 / 아니요)

   진행 중...

   죄송하지만, 거래가 거절되었습니다.

   잔액을 확인하세요.

H: 뭐가 잘못된 거야? 내 카드가 안 되는데.

H: 다른 데서 해 보자.

H: 다행이다!

42 # Police Stations 경찰서 p.186

P: 뭘 도와드릴까요? / H: 신고하러 왔어요.

P: 무슨 일이 있었는지 설명해 주시겠어요? / H: 한국어를 못해요.

H: 영어 하는 분 있어요? / C: 아니요.

H: 대사관에 연락해 주세요.

43 # Clinics 병원 p.190

M: 지금 진료받을 수 있어요? 응급 상황이에요.

N: 이 양식을 먼저 작성해 주세요.

1. 나이

2. 혈액형

3. 병력

   _고혈압

   _당뇨

   _천식

   _심장병

   _기타

4. 여성인 경우만

   임신 중 (예 / 아니요)

5. 복용하는 약이 있습니까? (예 / 아니요)

   '예'를 선택했으면, 여기에 상세한 내용을 적으세요.

44 # Pharmacies 약국 p.192

M: 괜찮아요? / H: 아니요, 어지러워요.

M: 열 있어요? / H: 네. 독감 걸린 거 같아요.

M: 언제부터요? / H: 어제요. / M: 약국에 가요.

P: 안녕하세요. 어디가 불편해요? / H: 두통이 약간 있어요.

P: 이거 드세요, 하루에 세 번이요.

M: 좀 쉬어요! / H: 네, 고마워요.

45 # Greetings 인사 p.202

H: 안녕하세요! 잘 지내요?

M: 잘 지내요, 당신은요? / H: 저도 잘 지내요.

H: 잘 가요! / M: 안녕히 가세요!

H: 잘 지내요! / M: 연락해요.

46 # Introductions 소개

p.204

M: 마이클이라고 합니다. 이름이 뭐예요? / H: 헤더입니다.

M: 어디 출신이에요? / H: 미국이요.

H: 직업이 뭐예요? / M: 엔지니어예요. 당신은요?

H: 학생이에요.

47 # Giving Thanks 감사하기

p.206

H: 고마워요! / M: 천만에요.

H: 매우 감사해요! / M: 뭘요.

M: 정말 감사합니다! / H: 제가 기뻐요.

H: 정말 친절하세요. / M: 별말씀을요.

48 # Apologies 사과
p.208

H: 늦었네요. 죄송합니다. / M: 괜찮습니다.

H: 그건 정말 미안합니다.

M: 사과할게요. / H: 별거 아니에요.

M: 제 잘못이에요. / H: 걱정하지 마세요.

49 # Requests 요청
p.210

H: 저기요. / M: 잠시만요.

M: 무슨 일이세요? / H: 좀 도와주세요!

M: 부탁 좀 해도 될까요? / H: 물론이죠.

M: 좀 비켜 주세요. / H: 네.

50 # Confirming Information 정보 확인 p.212

M: 한국에 갈 거예요. / H: 뭐라고요?

M: 한국에 간다고요. / H: 아, 좋겠어요.

H: 근데, 정말이에요? / M: 네.

H: 농담이죠? / M: 아니요. 진짜예요.

H: 와! 즐거운 여행되세요!

51 # Emotions 감정 p.214

M: 네!

H: 대단해!

M: 놀라워!

H: 완벽해!

M: 좋아!

M: 아니요!

H: 세상에!

M: 끔찍해!

H: 조용히 해!